In Defense of Politics
in Public Administration

Public Administration: Criticism & Creativity

Series Editor
Camilla Stivers

Editorial Advisory Board
Thomas J. Catlaw
Terry L. Cooper
David J. Farmer
Martha Feldman
Cynthia J. McSwain
David H. Rosenbloom
Peregrine Schwartz-Shea
Michael W. Spicer
Orion F. White, Jr.

In Defense of Politics
in Public Administration

A Value Pluralist Perspective

Michael W. Spicer

THE UNIVERSITY OF ALABAMA PRESS
Tuscaloosa

Typeface: Garamond

∞

The paper on which this book is printed meets the minimum requirements of
American National Standard for Information Sciences-Permanence of Paper
for Printed Library Materials, ANSI Z39.48-1984.

Library of Congress Cataloging-in-Publication Data

Spicer, Michael W.
In defense of politics in public administration : a value pluralist perspective /
Michael W. Spicer.
p. cm. — (Public administration : criticism and creativity)
Includes bibliographical references.
ISBN 978-0-8173-1685-3 (cloth : alk. paper) 1. Public administration.
2. Pluralism. 3. Political science—Philosophy. I. Title.
JF1351.S584 2010
351.01—dc22

2009026106

To my mother, Annie Doreen Tavernor

Contents

Preface

This book seeks to provide a defense for the practice of politics in public administration. Notwithstanding the sometimes shabby reputation of politics, not just among citizens but also among many academics, I argue here that politics is crucial to protecting the array of conflicting values or conceptions of the good that constitute our moral experience as human beings, both in our private lives and in the conduct of government and public administration. Politics does this, albeit in an imperfect fashion, because it encourages political leaders and public administrators to respond to the conflicting views of different groups of citizens in our society, because it allows some measure of personal freedom to us as we go about making our own choices among conflicting values, and also because it helps to maintain some sort of a peace among us as we make these choices. I have come to believe that defending politics is especially important nowadays because of a renewed enthusiasm among so many in our field for a more scientific approach to the study of governance and public administration—an approach, in my view, that is problematic because it downplays the conflict and uncertainty that are characteristic of the deeply political way in which we have come to govern ourselves. Therefore, what I also seek to offer here is an alternative approach to governance and public administration, an approach that properly recognizes that governance is inherently political in that it is concerned with the peaceful resolution of conflict among competing ends or conceptions of the good, an approach that also recognizes that, because governance is political, public administrators will often be faced with making choices among such ends without recourse to any sort of scientific algorithm and that they have a moral responsibility for these choices.

In writing this book, I have drawn on a wide variety of different philosophical, as well as historical, sources. I owe a special intellectual debt here to the ideas of Isaiah Berlin, Bernard Crick, and Stuart Hampshire. What I try to do in this book, as in much of my previously published work, is to introduce readers to a variety of what I believe are interesting conversations going on in philosophy and history and then use these conversations to draw what I think are some useful insights into public administration enquiry and practice. This may explain why, as readers may notice, I make extensive use of quotations so that the reader may get the flavor of the conversations by hearing the participants speak in their own words. My hope here is that, whether or not readers happen to agree with my arguments, they, nonetheless, may derive some enjoyment and value from hearing these conversations themselves.

I would like to thank publishers of my previous work for permission to reprint, in this book, portions of the text from the following articles written by me: "Politics and the Limits of a Science of Governance: Some Reflections on the Thought of Bernard Crick," *Public Administration Review* 67.4 (2007): 768–79, copyright © 2007 by Blackwell Publishers Inc.; and "Determinism, Social Science, and Public Administration: Lessons from Isaiah Berlin," *American Review of Public Administration* 35.3 (2005): 256–69, copyright © 2005 by Sage Publications, reprinted by permission of Sage Publications. This book also draws on ideas and text that originally appeared in two of my other articles: "Value Pluralism and Its Implications for American Public Administration," *Administrative Theory and Praxis* 23.4 (2001): 507–38; "Public Administration Enquiry and Social Science in the Postmodern Condition," *Administrative Theory and Praxis* 27.4 (2005): 669–88. In most cases, the text taken from these articles has been divided up among several chapters of this book, and all have been extensively revised.

Furthermore, I would like to thank my colleagues at Cleveland State University, the Public Administration Theory Network, and the American Society for Public Administration, as well as Mark Rutgers and his colleagues at the University of Leiden, for their generous assistance to me, over the past few years, in thinking through my ideas for this book. Special thanks are due to David Rosenbloom and to Camilla Stivers, as well as the anonymous reviewers, whose assistance in looking over an earlier draft of the manuscript did much to improve the quality of the book and whose encouragement helped me to keep at it. Conversations with all of these kind and talented "fellow travelers" in public administration contributed immeasurably to the development of this book, although, of course, none of them are responsible for any errors, omissions, or other shortcomings that might remain in the final text of the book. Thanks are also due to Cleveland State University for providing me with the academic leave and other resources necessary to undertake this project. Finally, special thanks are due to my wife, Claudia, who patiently listened to my ideas and provided me with candid feedback on my prose as I put pen to paper, and who, drawing on her skills as a librarian, helped me prepare the index for this book.

In Defense of Politics
in Public Administration

I
Introduction

Anti-Politics in Public Administration

The purpose of this book is to offer a defense for the idea and practice of politics in public administration. Admittedly, defending politics nowadays is a challenging task in light of the fact that politics and politicians are not especially popular and, in fact, candidates for elected office of a variety of ideological stripes often make great play of their desire to take politics out of government and to make government run more like a business or, alternatively, like a family or even a church. However, in looking at the failed states all around the world, this sort of antipathy towards politics strikes me as a rather silly, if not outright dangerous, sentiment. Certainly, like all human activities, politics reflects many of the vices that we see in much of human behavior: those of greed, avarice, pride, vanity, envy, lust, and so forth. Nonetheless, notwithstanding the vices of politics, it is important to remember that politics is also productive of certain virtues. Perhaps among the most important of these is that it can help us to keep the peace by limiting the use of violence in dealing with our differences. Whatever its vices, politics as a practice, for example, has enabled us in the United States, despite a wrenching depression and enduring racial strife, to avoid a second civil war for nearly a century and a half. Moreover, as events in Darfur, the Congo, and elsewhere make abundantly clear, keeping the peace through politics is not an achievement to be sneezed at. The horrific events of human suffering and violence associated with these conflicts should serve to remind us that politics is a precious, but also a very fragile, human achievement and it is not one lightly to be put aside. Politics provides us with a means of settling, at least for a time, the inevitable conflicts of interests and values or conceptions of the good that seem to arise among us without having constantly to take up arms against each other. Politics is, as Bernard Crick once wrote, "a way of ruling divided societies without undue violence" ([1962] 1993, 33). Moreover, as I argue in this book, politics is far more than just this. It is also a way of forcing us to face up to the conflicts among moral claims or values that are an integral part not just of our personal moral experience, but also of the practice of government and public administration. Furthermore, politics is a means of limiting the sometimes seductive and even admittedly occasionally helpful, but more often personally and socially destructive, consequences of single-minded obsession and zealotry.

Anti-Politics

Notwithstanding what I hope to demonstrate are these virtues of politics, it must be admitted that public administration, since its inception as a self-conscious field of study, has often expressed what can best be termed an "anti-political" attitude. Woodrow Wilson, for example, famously expressed such an attitude when he complained about the fact that "the people . . . have a score of differing opinions" and "can agree upon nothing simple" so that "advance must be made through compromise, by a compounding of differences, by a trimming of plans and a suppression of too straightforward principles" (1887, 207). In Wilson's view, politics was an obstacle to progress and reform because "the many, the people who are sovereign have no single ear which one can approach" and they "are selfish, ignorant, timid, stubborn, or foolish with the selfishnesses, the ignorances, the stubbornesses, the timidities, or the follies of several thousand persons" (1887, 208). More recently, Richard Nathan has complained about "the hyper-pluralism of American government" and has argued that we should consider ways of "toning down" this hyper-pluralism so that "hard problems can be addressed more easily and more expeditiously" and so that we might "get policy closure on high-salience issues and bring competence to bear in the implementation of these new policies once adopted" (1995, 215). Expressing an aversion to the political conflict characteristic of modern government, Nathan believes that we should do more to "insulate decisions from political heat and bring expertise to bear in doing so" (214). Nathan is by no means alone here in his aversion to political conflict. Kenneth Meier, perhaps one of our leading contemporary public management scholars, has opined that our "electoral branches of government have failed as deliberative institutions" and that their "policy failures . . . are legion" because they are unable to "resolve goal conflict with informed public policy" (1997, 196). As Meier sees it, what public administration and governance need today is "more bureaucracy and less democracy" (196). Robert Behn, another leading writer in public management, has urged public managers to "exercise leadership" and to "take initiative to correct" what he sees as "the current failures of our system of governance" (1998, 221)—failures that include, in his view, the fact that "elected chief executives rarely give clear directions to their agency managers," the tendency of legislatures to "give directions that are ambiguous and contradictory—and often unrealistic" (214), and the "political failure of our system of governance created by the power of factions" (218).

Lest it be thought that this somewhat disdainful attitude towards the normal practice of politics has been somehow confined to the pages of specialized academic journals, it is worth noting that such an attitude has also been evident in more popular writings on public management. In discussing possible reforms in the budgetary process in the 1990s, the National Performance Review (NPR) report, for example, asserted that the budget should reflect what it termed "the thoughtful planning of our public leaders" and should not simply be "the product of struggles among competing interests" (Gore 1993, 15). "Unfortunately," from the NPR's perspective, "the most deliberate planning is often subordinated to politics" (15). David Osborne and Peter Plastrik sound a similarly critical note when they complain about how "steering" or "choosing and evaluating strategies to achieve fundamental goals" is "far easier in a rational, nonpoliticized environment than in the typical political environment one finds," because "in most political environments, elected officials are far more interested in achieving their short-term political goals . . . than in increasing the government's capacity to choose long-term goals and strategies to achieve them" (1997, 107). Indeed, these authors would seem to display an almost complete lack of any respect at all for the political process when they endorse the idea that government reformers should "stand up to the interests that block change" by pursuing a "damn the torpedoes, full speed ahead" approach to political and administrative reform (329). More recently, writing with Peter Hutchinson, Osborne urges reformers to reject "compromise policies" because "they do not produce the right outcome for the public at the end of the day" (2004, 334). In their view, it is time for reformers "to move beyond the outworn ideologies of left and right" and to seek "radical change rooted in common sense" (xiii–xiv).

The antipathy of our field to politics is exemplified best, perhaps, in the idea of the politics-administration dichotomy. Wilson, who is often credited with first advancing this idea, wanted public administration to be "removed from the hurry and strife of politics" (1887, 209). According to Wilson, "administration lies outside the proper sphere of politics" and "administrative questions are not political questions" (210). Civil service reform, for him, was "clearing the moral atmosphere of official life by establishing the sanctity of public office as a public trust" and was "but a moral preparation for what [was] to follow" (210). Seeking to further insulate administration from politics, Wilson sought the development of what he saw as an apolitical science of administration—one that, drawing on insights from European administrative theorists and the practices of European absolutist monarchies, would "straighten the paths of government, . . . make its business less unbusinesslike, . . . strengthen and purify its organization, and . . . crown its duties with dutifulness" (201).

Wilson's idea of a politics-administration dichotomy, despite being frequently discredited by critics such as Dwight Waldo ([1948] 1984) and Norton Long (1949), remains influential within our field. Waldo himself refers here to the "perdurability" of the politics-administration dichotomy (1983, 219) and, according to David Rosenbloom, the dichotomy "continues to define a good deal of administrative thought" (1993, 503). Contemporary popular writers on public management, for example, call for a separation of "policy decisions (steering) from service delivery (rowing)" (Osborne and Gaebler 1993, 35), a distinction that clearly parallels the dichotomy. Also, scholars such as James Svara and Patrick Overeem continue to debate the meaning, relevance, and implications of the dichotomy in the most recent pages of our scholarly journals (Svara 2006, 2008; Overeem 2006, 2008). As Gerald Caiden put the matter a quarter century ago, "the prospect of separating things political from things administrative remains enticing" (1984, 51). If the politics-administration dichotomy is a myth, as critics have often charged, then it is a myth that, at least for some, "still remains an ideal that may yet be attained," a myth that "will linger on as long as there remains a strong anti-politics flavor in American society and scholars and public professionals still strive for objectivity in public administration" and, also, "as long as there are people who would like to run society, any society, 'scientifically and objectively'" (Caiden 1984, 71).

Common to a great deal of our literature is the sentiment, therefore, that politics is, at best, a necessary intrusion into governance and administration and one that compromises its efficiency and effectiveness. There is the intimation in a lot of our literature that while, given our democratic ideals, we would of course never wish to do away entirely with the conflict, compromise, and uncertainty of politics, it would perhaps be better if we could have somewhat less of it and somewhat more of enlightened statesmanship, expert administration, or some combination of these. Camilla Stivers is correct, in my view, in recognizing here our "tendency to view politics as a contaminant of rational, rigorous practice" (2008, 56). Politics bashing is an age-old activity, one that dates back at least to the writings of Plato. We must recognize that politics and politicians have always had a somewhat shabby reputation. As Crick reminds us, there are "many who think that politics is muddled, contradictory, self-defeatingly recurrent, unprogressive, unpatriotic, inefficient, mere compromise, or even a sham or conspiracy" (1993, 16). Indeed, he notes how, for many people, "it is the first test of a new acquaintance's sensibility that he despises politics, politicians, and political speculation (even occasionally among those who 'profess' the subject). . . . They object to its most characteristic features—compromise, uncertainty, conflict" (165).

Nonetheless, there is reason to worry, in my view, when those who would seek to advise and educate our public policy-makers and administrators so often express what is clearly an anti-political attitude. There is a danger here that the public administrators we help train might internalize such an attitude and actually come to see themselves as somehow superior to, or above, politics. Crick recognizes this danger when he warns of "those who think that administration can always be clearly separated from politics, and that if this is done, there is really very little, if anything, that politicians can do that administrators cannot do better." This is "the view of the servant who would not merely be equal, but who would be master, or of the administrator who feels constantly frustrated in *his* work by the interventions of politicians" (1993, 107).

Science in Place of Politics

A major reason why a defense of politics in administration would seem especially important right now is that our discipline is showing a renewed interest in a more scientific approach to governance and public management (Meier 1997; Gill and Meier 2000; Lynn, Heinrich, and Hill 2000; Hill and Lynn 2004). As with antipathy towards politics, this enthusiasm for a science of governance is not an entirely new sentiment in public administration. As noted above, Wilson himself, early on in our field, sought the development of a science of administration that would, as he put it, discover "what government can properly and successfully do" (1887, 197). Indeed, because of the compromise, uncertainty, and conflict so often associated with politics throughout history, there have always been those who have been tempted by the possibility of some more rational, more scientific way of resolving the differences that arise among us. Among the best known of these was, perhaps, Henri de Saint-Simon, a French utopian positivist philosopher of the early nineteenth century, whose ideas influenced Karl Marx among others. Following the French Revolution and more than a decade of European war, Saint-Simon looked to positivist science to preserve peace and social order. He saw such science as the means of "stopping [the] terrible scourge of general war, and of reorganizing the European community" (1964, 27). The problem, in Saint-Simon's view, was that, because "the method of the sciences of observation has not been introduced into political questions, every man has imported his point of view, method of reasoning and judging, and hence there is not yet any precision in the answers, or universality in the results" (40). He believed that "divisions of [political] opinion arise from the fact that each man has too narrow a view" and that, "for clear thinking men, there is only one method of reasoning, only one way of seeing things, if they are looking at them from the same point of view" (67). Positivist science would remove the sources of war and political conflict in human affairs.

To avert revolution and anarchy in the future, Saint-Simon advanced a collectivist plan of radical political and social reform rooted in his concept of positivist science. He argued that "the main energies of the community . . . should be directed to the improvement of our moral and physical welfare" (1964, 76). In order to accomplish this end, Saint-Simon advocated giving "priority in State expenditure to ensuring work for all fit men, to secure their physical existence; spreading throughout the proletarian class a knowledge of positive science; ensuring for this class forms of recreation and interests which will develop their intelligence" (77). These efforts were to be administered by an elite group consisting of those "most fitted to manage the affairs of the nation, . . . [its] scientists, artists and industrialists" whose work "contributes most to national prosperity" (78). Saint-Simon saw the development of scientific knowledge as forming the basis for a non-deist "New Christianity," one that would "link together the scientists, artists, and industrialists, . . . make them the managing directors of the human race, as well as of the particular interests of each individual people," and "put the arts, experimental sciences and industry in the front rank of sacred studies" (105).

For Saint-Simon, social conflict and strife, both between nations and within nations, appeared as solely a technical problem, one that could be resolved on the basis of principles of positivist science and with the assistance of relevant expertise. To modern ears, Saint-Simon's ideas may seem wildly utopian, a mere philosopher's fantasy, at least at first glance. Nonetheless, this idea that social conflict might somehow be resolved by the application of science has remained very seductive. In fact, it is an idea that has pervaded an awful lot of our public administration literature and arguably forms the very foundation of our field. It appeared most visibly in the beginnings of our field in the scientific management movement of the early twentieth century, a movement that was inspired by the writings of Frederick Taylor. Taylor saw his principles of scientific management as not just a means of greatly enhancing economic prosperity, but also as a tool for resolving the great social conflicts of his time, most notably the industrial conflicts that were prevalent between workers and businesses of the early twentieth century. In fact, as Waldo observes in his classic review of early public administration writings, "it was the need for 'solidarity' that stimulated Taylor's first researches" (1984, 52). According to Waldo, Taylor disliked "the constant warfare" that he experienced as a foreman in supervising workers and "he wanted to take the matter of a fair day's work out of the realm of dispute" and "make the facts sovereign" (52). As Taylor himself wrote, scientific management was to render economic life not only "far more prosperous" but also "far happier, and more free from discord and dissension" ([1911] 1998, 11). He believed that the application of his scientific management principles would promote "more than all other causes, the close, intimate cooperation, the constant personal contact" between workers and businesses and, as a result, would "tend to diminish friction and discontent" (75). As Taylor saw it, "it is difficult for two people whose interests are the same, and who work side by side in accomplishing the same object, all day long, to keep up a quarrel" (75). Scientific management would reduce industrial conflict because it would arrange "mutual relations" between workers and businesses in such a way that "their interests become identical" (1). It was about "harmony, not discord," about "cooperation, not individualism" (74).

Taylor's ideas of scientific management are often closely associated with industry time management studies. However, Taylor saw his principles of scientific management as extending well beyond the shop floor of industry. In his view, these principles could be applied "with equal force to all social activities" including "the management of our homes; the management of our farms; the management of the business of our tradesmen, large and small; of our churches, our philanthropic institutions, our universities, and our governmental departments" (1998, iv). Taylor's followers were often even more effusive than he in regard to the potential contributions that scientific management might make to governance and society. Harlow Person, for example, believed that the philosophy, principles, and techniques of scientific management could be applied to the "conservation problems of entire nations, and perhaps of an entire world" (1972, xvi). Scientific management, for Taylor's disciples, was more than just a theory of management, as it is so often described nowadays in management textbooks. It was a moral, political, and social movement. Notwithstanding some acknowledgements that there might be realms of behavior where scientific management was inapplicable, there was within the scientific management movement, nonetheless, "a disposition to extend the discipline to the whole realm of political or economic behavior" (Waldo 1984, 55). In fact, some of Taylor's followers envisioned "the entire world run on the principles of scientific management: universal peace between nations, and between social classes, the ultimate in efficiency and in material satisfactions, liberty and equality in their proper portions, general education and enlightenment" (Waldo 1984, 52). As with Saint-Simon, there was also among Taylor and his followers, then, this same utopian inclination to substitute the principles of a science for politics in resolving social conflict. As Robert Kanigel writes in his recent biography of Taylor, for Taylor and his disciples "democracy . . . didn't mean argument, negotiation, debate, voting, or strikes. For science was at the helm now, consigning such cumbersome baggage to the past" (1997, 510). Scientific management was going to accomplish the social harmony that politics had failed to provide. It was "apolitical, even above politics. It was against social disharmony and unethical conduct and for justice, peace, cooperation, prosperity, and happiness" (Caiden 1984, 59).

Despite the blow that fascism and World War II dealt to this idea of a science of politics, there were, even in the postwar years, more than a few public administration scholars who were still quite willing to entertain this utopian idea that science might substitute for politics in the resolution of social conflict. Elton Mayo, one of the founders of what has often been termed the "human relations" approach to management, complained that "modern civilization for approximately two centuries has done nothing to extend and develop human cooperative capacities" and that, as a result, "civilization faces the latter part of the twentieth century divided into groups with few bonds of general unity, mutually suspicious, ready at any moment to develop mutual hatreds at the touch of an irresponsible orator or politician" (1945, 116–17). Mayo saw "society, within the nation and without it," as "breaking down into groups that show an ever-increasing hostility to each other; irrational hates . . . taking the place of cooperation, . . . the precursor of downfall for many valiant civilizations" (119). The remedy for this problem was "a new type of administrator," one "able to understand the human-social facts for what they actually are, unfettered by his own emotion or prejudice" and with "careful training" not simply in "relevant technical skills," but, more importantly, in the "organization of cooperation," a subject that Mayo felt had unfortunately been "ignored in universities, in industries, and in political statements" (122). Mayo looked to the careful and detailed study of human cooperation "to lead us out of the chaos of misery and malice that has overtaken our once proud civilization" (123).

Harold Lasswell, an early pioneer in the area of public policy studies, argued in a similar vein that the "roots of tension within our civilization" were to be found in "studying the psychotic, neurotic, and psychopathic manifestations of distorted development" and in discovering "the way in which specific patterns of culture warp the growth of congenial and productive interpersonal relations" (1951, 8). Once discovered and exposed, such "sources of human destructiveness" could be changed and "the basis [then] laid for a profound reconstruction of culture by continual study and not by . . . the traditional methods of political agitation" (8). In his book on *Psychopathology and Politics* ([1930] 1986), Lasswell argued more specifically that what was needed was a "politics of prevention." In Lasswell's words, "the time has come to abandon the assumption that the problem of politics is the problem of promoting discussion among all the interests concerned in a given problem. Discussion frequently complicates social difficulties, for the discussion by far-flung interests arouses a psychology of conflict which produces obstructive, fictitious, and irrelevant values. The problem of politics is less to solve conflicts than to prevent them; less to serve as a safety valve for social protest than to apply social energy to the abolition of recurrent sources of strain in society" (196–97). This politics of prevention, in his view, would draw "attention squarely to the central problem of strain and maladaptation in society" (197). It would rely on the "education of social administrators and social scientists" and would "be intimately allied to general medicine, psychopathology, physiological psychology, and related disciplines" (203).

Science as an Aid to Politics

In the past half century, the idea that science might actually replace the practice of politics has undoubtedly receded somewhat. Perhaps this is because the social and behavioral sciences have simply not been up to the job. They have proven unable to provide reliable remedies for resolving the various conflicts that divide us as human beings. Nonetheless, there remain those who believe that, if science cannot actually substitute for politics, it can at least make significant improvements to the way in which we govern ourselves. This idea of better governance through science has been urged on us again, in recent years, with a certain zeal by writers in the area of what has come to be termed public management. Laurence Lynn, for example, one of the more prominent and accomplished of these writers, takes our field to task for its failure "to engage in empirical validation in any scientific sense" and also for its lack of "theory-building traditions . . . analogous to those of either the disciplines or the well-established professions" (1996, 164). For Lynn, "engaging in empirical validation of predictions, conjectures, and statements is central to any scholarly activity directed at professional performance" (164). Writing with Carolyn Hill, more recently, he observes how we need to use "the formal theories, models, methods, and data of the social and behavioral sciences to study governmental processes" so as to "develop a body of empirical knowledge concerning what works and why" (Hill and Lynn 2004, 5). Also, Jeff Gill and Kenneth Meier have set forth what they boldly choose to term a "methodological manifesto" for our field, arguing that "public administration research has fallen notably behind research in related fields in terms of methodological sophistication" (2000, 157), and that what we need is "a greatly enhanced focus on empiricism and rigorous quantitative approaches" (195).

What is most notable about these recent crusaders for a scientifically more rigorous public administration is that they seek to transcend the shopworn politics-administration dichotomy and urge us to adopt a more scientific approach to the study and practice, not simply of the administration of particular agencies, but of entire systems of governance. Laurence Lynn, Carolyn Heinrich, and Carolyn Hill, for example, see social science research as needing to address what they believe is the "general issue of governance," namely, how "public-sector regimes, agencies, programs, and activities [can] be organized and managed to achieve public purposes" (2000, 234). In their view, this is an issue that should be of concern to "officials in all branches and at all levels of the public sector: legislators, elected and appointed executives, and judges at federal, state, and local levels of government" (234). Kenneth Meier expresses a similarly expansive view of a social science approach to public administration when he argues that we need to "redefine the field of public administration to encompass the design, evaluation, and implementation of institutions and public policy" (1997, 194). Seeking to extend the ideas of Herbert Simon, he argues that public administration research should become "*the* science of the artificial for both politics and administration" (195). In short, these authors seek to use the techniques of mainstream quantitative social science to answer not merely managerial questions but also the broad types of political questions that have managed to preoccupy and puzzle political philosophers and observers for centuries, if not millennia.

In Defense of Politics

In light of this renewed enthusiasm among public management writers for the application of social science to both the design and operation of our systems of governance, as well as the longstanding antipathy towards politics in our field, a defense of politics in administration therefore would seem especially timely, and that is why I have written this book. I argue here that the practice of politics is useful, if not actually necessary, to the moral conduct of government and public administration. This is because it serves to protect the value pluralism or moral conflict that is an integral part of our moral experience as human beings. In this book, I examine the idea of value pluralism and the role that politics plays in helping to protect value pluralism in political discourse and practice within a political community. In doing so, I draw, in significant part, upon the writings of Isaiah Berlin, Stuart Hampshire, and Bernard Crick, all of whom understood the character of value conflict and its close relationship to politics. The implications of this analysis for public administration will be examined. It is argued here that public administrators need to go beyond the science-based instrumental rationalism and determinism that characterize too much of our field and to recognize that the management of conflicting values is an essential part of their responsibilities. Also, I explore how administrators might learn from the adversary reasoning that is characteristic of the political process and incorporate it, more self-consciously, into their own decision making.

Chapter 2 of this book begins the argument by examining Berlin's idea of value pluralism and how this pluralism is central to our moral experience, both in making our own moral choices among conflicting moral ends or conceptions of the good and in living with others whose moral ends happen to differ from ours. It is argued here that, far from being a form of relativism, value pluralism is an essential part of our moral experience and that in fact, without it, morality and moral choices, at least as we have come to understand them, would disappear. This chapter also emphasizes the importance of moral conflict to decision making in government and public administration and its special relevance to the problem of the "dirty hands" dilemma in government.

Chapter 3 uses the writings of Crick to examine the historical meaning and function of politics and shows the special role of politics in helping us to deal with moral conflicts in a manner that minimizes the need for force and violence. I argue here that politics helps to promote moral conduct because it encourages governments to be responsive to a variety of different values or conceptions of the good held by different groups in society. Politics also makes it easier for individuals and groups in society to pursue their own values because it allows individuals a measure of freedom from government interference and because it helps to promote a more peaceful coexistence among these individuals and groups.

Following this, in chapter 4 I examine the conflict that exists between politics and the vision of governance proposed by mainstream social scientists in public administration and especially by writers in public management. I argue here that a scientific approach to the study of governance, when taken alone, gives insufficient weight to its inherently political character because it advances an instrumental rationalist and deterministic vision of governance and, in doing so, downplays the conflicts of values and the uncertainty that are an inherent part of the way in which we have come to govern ourselves. As a result, this approach to governance may not be as helpful to the practice of public administration or governance as its advocates seem to think. Moreover, there is a risk that if public administrators and other government officials were to embrace this science-based approach too enthusiastically, to the point of excluding other more humanistic approaches, it could even harm the practice of governance. The chapter concludes that what we need is a pluralist approach to public administration that takes account of the political character of our system of governance and that recognizes that public administrators must often make choices among competing values.

Chapter 5 explores just what such a pluralist approach to public administration might look like by examining more closely how it is that politics is able to reconcile conflicts among groups holding rival conceptions of the good. Drawing on the ideas of Hampshire, it is argued here that political institutions can provide a set of locally accepted practices of procedural justice that help to resolve conflict by means of adversarial argument or "hearing the other side" rather than by force. This suggests, in the American context, the particular relevance of our constitutional practices in dealing with moral conflict. I argue here that our constitutional and political practices have led to a politicization of public administration that makes it difficult, if not impossible, for administrators to act in an apolitical or purely instrumental rationalist fashion and, furthermore, has the effect of forcing public administrators to take account of multiple and conflicting perspectives in making their decisions. In doing so, these practices serve to protect values that are held to be important by different groups in society by providing multiple opportunities for hearing the other side on issues involving these values. The protection and enhancement of these practices for hearing the other side is, therefore, a necessary part of a pluralist approach to public administration.

Finally, chapter 6 examines how the process of adversarial argument or hearing the other side that is characteristic of politics might help public administrators engage in a process of practical moral reasoning as part of a pluralist approach to public administration. It is argued here that a more self-conscious cultivation within the mind of an internalized process of adversary reasoning—one that is derived from our social practices for resolving moral conflict—can be useful to public administrators in both thinking about and dealing more effectively with conflicting values. I also argue here that public administrators can engage more effectively in this type of practical moral reasoning by drawing upon the type of rationality that is reflected in legal arguments and upon the imaginative skills that can be fostered by reading literature and history.

Methodological Approach

The methodology employed in this book might best be described as a "history of ideas." Berlin, himself a self-professed student of the history of ideas, once described this as the "history of what we believe that people thought and felt" (Berlin and Jahanbegloo 1991, 28). This involves, for him, an examination of "beliefs, attitudes and mental and emotional habits, some of which are vague and undefined, others of which have become crystallised into religious, legal or political systems, moral doctrines, social outlooks, psychological dispositions and so forth" (Berlin 2000, 69). Similarly, for Roger Hausheer, the history of ideas can be seen as an attempt, among other things, "to trace the birth and development of some of the ruling concepts of a civilization or culture through long periods of mental change, and to reconstruct the image men have of themselves and their activities, in a given age and culture" (1982, xvii). It includes an examination of the basic ideas or concepts in terms of which men and women "have seen themselves and framed their aspirations" (xvi).

The purpose of such an enquiry is to attempt to understand some of the basic categories, concepts, or patterns that all of us, including social scientists, have come to use in making sense of human experience and, especially, those aspects of human experience concerned with politics and governance. Some of these categories are more permanent and some of them are more transitory. Some of them are more universal in the sense that they seem to appear across different cultures whereas others are more local. However, together these categories form the "spectacles" or lenses through which we look at the facts or data of human actions and experience. They involve notions such as "society, freedom, sense of time and change, suffering, happiness, productivity, good and bad, right and wrong, choice, effort, truth, illusion" (Berlin 1979, 166). By understanding these categories, we can gain an awareness of both the factual and normative presuppositions that undergird our perceptions, beliefs, attitudes, and values.

As a field of enquiry, public administration has, of course, from time to time drawn on the history of ideas for insight, including a few early writers in public administration such as Woodrow Wilson and Frank Goodnow. In recent years, a number of contemporary writers such as John Rohr (1986), Richard Stillman (1998), and Camilla Stivers (2000a) have also demonstrated how an examination of the history of political and social ideas can be helpful to the study and practice of contemporary public administration. Nonetheless, it remains true that, at least among our mainstream public administration writers, there is a marked tendency to downplay the importance of the history of political and social ideas in public administration enquiry. In this respect, many of them would still seem to follow the lead of Lyndall Urwick, who wrote in the 1930s that human organizations or administrative systems can be examined without regard to "any constitutional, political or social theory underlying [their] creation" (1937, 49). This tendency to de-emphasize political and social ideas is evident in recent years, for example, among contemporary writers in the so-called reinventing government or new public management movement. These writers argue that the problems of government are managerial rather than political or ideological, and that the solution to these problems is a more entrepreneurial approach to public administration rather than new public policies or, for that matter, new political institutions. Reinventing government, for them, is both politically and ideologically neutral. It is about "*how* government should work," not "*what* it should do" (Gore 1993, ii), and its principles are applicable "regardless of party, regardless of ideology" (6). Furthermore, these principles can be applied universally across all kinds of political systems with quite different political ideologies and traditions. As these writers see it, their strategies "work in small cities and large nations, in parliamentary systems and presidential systems, in strong mayor cities and council-manager cities" (Osborne and Plastrik 1997, 44). Different types of political systems and organizations may require different tactics, in their view, but "none of these differences changes the basic levers that create fundamental change" so that "reinvention applies to all types of organizations" (47). Implicit in the rhetoric of these writers is the idea that any enquiry into the history of political and social ideas is relatively unimportant—if not actually irrelevant—to public administration. Indeed, the very terms "reinventing government" and "new public management" strongly intimate the irrelevance of such a history.

Nonetheless, in my view, an examination of the history of ideas, especially moral and political ideas, is not only desirable but also essential to understanding public administration. This is because, despite the aforementioned indifference of many scholars in the field to broad and abstract moral and political ideas, such ideas permeate the categories or presuppositions that we bring to the examination of the facts of human experience and action in government. Much as we might try, we cannot shut them out, since they shape the very language we use to describe these facts. As Mark Rutgers has reminded us in his recent article on comparative public administration, the meanings of the words that we employ in this vocabulary are always "embedded in specific conceptual and cultural (legal, historical and political) backgrounds" (2004, 151). The meanings of words like public administration, government, constitution, law, democracy, citizen, and legislature are inextricably connected through our mental frameworks to what it is that we think government does, can do, or ought to do. Also, at a deeper level, the meanings that we attach to these words are tied to our notions of morality and what we think of as being human. In this sense, one cannot think, talk, or write about human beings as such in the absence of moral considerations, because the concept of what it means to be a human being is inevitably suffused with value judgments of some sort or other. Of course, a degree of evenhandedness may be possible and is certainly desirable, but neutrality itself is simply not a realistic option for us. Indeed, as Berlin observes, we can rarely, if ever, "achieve neutrality" in statements about "moral and social life" because the words we must employ in making such statements are "inescapably charged with ethical or aesthetic or political content" (1979, 157). In the study of history, for example, valuations—"moral, political, aesthetic"—are "intrinsic . . . to the subject matter" (Berlin 1969, 92), and "our historical language, the words and thoughts with which we attempt to reflect about or describe past events and persons, embody moral concepts and categories" (95). As Berlin notes, in thinking about the harm done by Adolf Hitler, for instance, "the very use of normal language cannot avoid conveying what the author regards as commonplace or monstrous, decisive or trivial, exhilarating or depressing. In describing what occurred, I can say that so many million men were brutally done to death; or alternatively, that they perished; laid down their lives; were massacred; or simply, that the population of Europe was reduced, or that its average age was lowered; or that many men lost their lives. None of these descriptions of what took place is wholly neutral: all carry moral implications" (xxix).

In other words, we cannot help but use moral and political ideas when thinking about human experience and action in government. This being the case, we should therefore at least try to be self-conscious when we do make use of these ideas. As Berlin puts it, "to neglect the field of political thought" is "merely to allow oneself to remain at the mercy of primitive and uncriticized political beliefs" (1969, 119). Waldo certainly understood the importance of such self-awareness within our field when he wrote in the 1980s that "the literature of public administration contains elements that are political theory as this is conventionally understood" and that "it serves useful functions to identify such elements and to examine them carefully: to trace their ancestry, to identify their analogs, to examine critically their intended explicit uses and their possible implicit functions in the political system" (1984, x). Waldo makes clear here how closely political and moral ideas are tied to the study and practice of public administration. Certainly, in his view, "there are limited, technical areas where public administrationists can escape, practically speaking, from concern with political theory; but, nevertheless, in their central concerns they cannot avoid this encounter. It is, rather, a matter of the level of consciousness and the degree of intelligence that is brought to the encounter" (lvii).

Greater self-awareness about moral and political ideas in public administration enquiry and education is something for which we ought to strive for a number of reasons. For one thing, if scholars in public administration, as well as the practitioners whom they help educate and train, do not bother to think about the moral and political ideas that undergird both past and present administrative ideas and practices, then both are likely to remain vulnerable to seduction by ideas and reforms that are really not as new as they appear to be, but, to the contrary, have often been tried before and found wanting. For example, administrative reforms that would have us run our system of governance and administration more like a business enterprise or corporation, reforms such as reinventing government and, before it, such reforms as program budgeting, zero-base budgeting, and MBO, arise in the United States over and over again as if, each time, they were entirely new and unrelated to any intellectual traditions in our past. Were scholars and practitioners to pay more attention to the history of ideas, they might become more aware of and sensitive to the problems and pitfalls that have beset the efforts of past political and administrative reformers. They might be less susceptible to the superficial novelty of such ideas as "entrepreneurial" or "mission-driven" government and more inclined to look at them circumspectly. In this regard, an examination of the history of ideas can provide scholars and practitioners a richer intellectual context that can help them better evaluate administrative ideas and reforms. By providing such a context, an exposure to the history of our ideas can at least provide some partial protection, some degree of immunity, against the recurring fads or what Christopher Hood and Michael Jackson term "the administrative fashion, 'consultocracy,' . . . pop management," and "many incentives for amnesia" (1994, 484) that so often tend to infect our thinking and practice.

Moreover, unless we are self-conscious about the moral and political ideas that are intimated in our words, writings, and actions, then there is a danger that public administration—both as a field of study and a practice—may become susceptible to influence by ideas that are not simply somewhat unhelpful, but are actually destructive of values we have come to cherish. In doing so, given the way in which ideas can influence practice, if we neglect the history of our moral and political ideas, then we may risk more than simply disappointment. As Berlin rightly reminded us, "Men cannot live without seeking to describe and explain the universe to themselves. The models they use in doing this must deeply affect their lives, not least when they are unconscious; much of the misery and frustration of men is due to the mechanical or unconscious, as well as deliberate, application of models where they do not work" (1979, 10).

When he wrote these words, Berlin had in mind, of course, the abuses and horrors resulting from twentieth-century totalitarianism. However, the dangers of not paying enough attention to our moral and political ideas are by no means limited to societies ruled by totalitarian despots. Rosenbloom has warned us, for example, how, here in the United States, in their quest for keys to better and more cost-effective governance, "practitioners and public administration scholars have, at best, marginalized and, at worst, been contemptuous of democratic-constitutional values" (2007, 28). Detailing recent enhancements of executive power and various abuses of administrative power, including those at Abu Ghraib, Rosenbloom observes how "regardless of what drives today's administrative reformers—cost-effectiveness, business-like models, faith in executive power, social equity, accountability for results or other concerns—they infrequently focus on whether their prescriptions will promote or diminish individual rights, constitutional integrity, transparency, and the rule of law" (36).

For these reasons, it is thus incumbent upon those of us who think about, write about, and teach public administration to understand and appreciate better the history of our moral and political ideas. This is particularly important at a time when our field seems increasingly dominated by a narrow instrumental rationalism and scientism. It may be argued, of course, that the pursuit of such an approach to public administration enquiry and education may render it too theoretical and too far removed from the practical day-to-day concerns of public administrators. However, to assert this is to ignore the argument made here that the moral and political ideas which we expound in our writings and in our classes, whether consciously or unconsciously, exert an influence over the practice of public administration and governance. As my good friend the late Larry Terry once said, "those concerned with public management and practice must not lose sight of the fact that ideas matter; they do have consequences" (1998, 198).

2

Value Pluralism
and Moral Experience

The central argument of this book is that politics plays a crucial role in helping societies manage conflicts among different values or conceptions of the good. To understand better how politics plays this role, we must first understand and appreciate the idea of value pluralism. Put in its simplest terms, value pluralism is the idea that our moral values or conceptions of the good are many and varied and that we often find they come into conflict with one another in ways that do not permit any easy reconciliation or solution. This idea of value pluralism arguably can be traced back as far as the writings of the Greek philosopher Heraclitus (Hampshire 2000), who, recognizing the pervasiveness of conflict in human life, wrote some two and a half millennia ago, "the poet was a fool who wanted no conflict among us, gods or people" (Heraclitus 2001, 29). For Heraclitus, good and bad are inextricably tied together because "the cosmos works by harmony of tensions like the lyre and the bow" (37). However, it is the late Isaiah Berlin who perhaps deserves the most credit for raising awareness of the issue of value pluralism among contemporary philosophers. Berlin put the matter with his characteristic clarity and humanity of prose when he wrote some decades ago that the "ends of men are many, and not all of them are in principle compatible with one another" so that "the possibility of conflict—and of tragedy—can never wholly be eliminated from human life" (1969, 169). For Berlin, the fact that we are forced to choose between competing moral claims is "an inescapable characteristic of the human condition" (169). Since Berlin wrote, an increasing number of political theorists and philosophers have sought to explicate and to develop further this idea of value pluralism (see, for example, Hampshire 1983; Raz 1986; Lukes 1989; Kekes 1993; Gray 2000; Galston 2002). Drawing upon this literature, this chapter explores the meaning of value pluralism, as well as that of its antithesis, monism, and suggests why value pluralism provides a more truthful account of our moral experience than monism both in our private lives and in government.

The Meaning of Value Pluralism

In discussing the idea of value pluralism, philosophers have used a variety of different terminologies. Some talk quite explicitly about value pluralism as such; some, like Berlin, just talk about pluralism; and others, including Hampshire, simply talk about moral conflicts or conflicts among values or moral claims. However, while there may be subtle differences in emphasis, these philosophers all seem to be talking about essentially the same thing, namely, the idea described by Hampshire that we face "conflicting claims which are not to be settled by appeal to a criterion that is always overriding and final" (1983, 24). Hampshire's words reveal here what contemporary writers on pluralism have come to see as two important defining characteristics of value pluralism: first, the idea that certain of our values are incompatible or uncombinable with one another, and second, the idea that some of these may also turn out to be incommensurable or incomparable with one another. It will be helpful here to examine each of these characteristics in turn.

When we say that our values or moral ends are incompatible with one another, we mean here simply that the pursuit of certain values that we hold to be important must inevitably compromise or limit our ability to pursue certain other important values. The more we seek to attain some of these values, the less able we are to attain the others. Value incompatibility can be seen here as entailing what John Gray has termed "a thesis of *moral scarcity* as applied to the virtues" (1996, 44). This incompatibility arises because of the very nature of certain values, at least as we have come to understand them. It is due, as John Kekes puts it, to "qualities intrinsic to the conflicting values" (1993, 21). Berlin vividly captured the idea of value incompatibility when, in an interview, he observed that "some of the ultimate values by which men live cannot be reconciled or combined, not just for practical reasons, but in principle, conceptually. Nobody can be both a careful planner, and, at the same time, wholly spontaneous. You cannot combine full liberty with full equality—full liberty for the wolves cannot be combined with full liberty for the sheep. Justice and mercy, knowledge and happiness can collide" (Berlin and Jahanbegloo 1991, 142).

It is important to stress here that, from a value pluralist perspective, these conflicts among incompatible values or moral claims do not arise from ignorance, error, intellectual laziness, or, for that matter, human mendacity, notwithstanding the fact that these are all commonplace human weaknesses. They are not the type of conflicts that we might somehow be able to resolve in some way simply on the basis of either more thoughtful analysis or more sincere reflection. "We not only find these conflicts in our unreflective intuitions and in commonplace morality; we may also find, after reflection on the source and nature of our moral intuitions, that these conflicts are unavoidable and not to be softened or glossed over" (Hampshire 1983, 117).

Furthermore, it is also important to understand that these conflicts between incompatible values can occur at a variety of different levels. As Berlin notes, values can "easily clash within the breast of a single individual," but they can also be "incompatible between cultures, or groups in the same culture, or between you and me" (1992, 12). In other words, value conflicts can make themselves known at personal, interpersonal, intergroup, and intercultural levels. This multifaceted character of value conflict is important to recognize, because it means that value conflict presents individuals or groups with not simply a moral problem in terms of what they ought to do. It also presents them with a political problem in terms of how different individuals and groups, who happen to hold different and conflicting values, should live together. As Hampshire observes, "conflicts between conceptions of the good, moral conflicts" exist for us then "both in the soul and in the city" (2000, 5). These conflicts in the "city" arise because of the wide diversity of conceptions of the good that different human beings in different times and in different places seem capable of imagining. As Hampshire argues, "prominent among the essential potentialities of the human soul . . . is [its] capacity for linguistic, cultural and moral diversity" (1989, 30). As a result of this widely observed human capacity for diversity, "the description of ideal societies and ideal persons and ideal ways of life, and moral imagination . . . vary vastly in form and content in different places, in different social groups, at different times in history, and in distinguishable cultures" (Hampshire 2000, 20). Where different groups and cultures coexist within the same state or political community, it should not be surprising, therefore, that their different conceptions of the good will sometimes clash with one another so that "within any nation there will always be contests arising not only from conflicting interests, . . . but also from competing moral outlooks and entrenched beliefs" (79). As Hampshire notes, "our political enmities in the city or state will never come to an end while we have diverse life stories and diverse imaginations" (5).

The foregoing idea that certain among our values may be inherently in conflict or incompatible with one another may strike some readers as neither particularly surprising nor novel. After all, conflicts among values are recognized as commonplace in much of philosophical, social scientific, and ordinary discourse. However, more unsettling, and perhaps much more subversive, is the pluralist idea that many of these conflicting values can also turn out to be incommensurable with one another. What is meant by incommensurability among values is that there is no single criterion to which we might appeal in order to resolve value conflicts in a fully rational manner. As George Crowder has noted, such incommensurability "implies that there is no *summum bonum* or supervalue in terms of which all other values can be quantified, and weighed against one another" (1994, 295). More precisely, where there is incommensurability among values, this means, as Stephen Lukes argues, that "there is no single currency or scale on which conflicting values can be measured, and that where a conflict occurs no rationally compelling appeal can be made to some value that will resolve it. Neither is superior to the other, nor are they equal in value" (1989, 135). Incommensurability deprives us, therefore, of "an infallible measuring rod," one that might certify "one form of life as being superior to all others" (Berlin 1982, 70). It means that we cannot "represent moral decision as an operation which a slide rule could, in principle, perform" (Berlin 1969, 171).

To look at this, perhaps, in another way, to believe that values or moral ends are incommensurable with one another is to accept the notion of what Richard Rorty has called, somewhat playfully, "polytheism." As he puts it, "You are a polytheist if you think that there is no actual or possible object of knowledge that would permit you to commensurate and rank all human needs. . . . To be a polytheist in this sense you do not have to believe [as did the pre-Socratic Greeks] that there are non-human persons with power to intervene in human affairs. All you need do is abandon the idea that we should try to find a way of making everything hang together, which will tell all human beings what to do with their lives, and tell all of them the same thing" (2007, 30).

Incommensurability among certain values clearly places severe limits on the role that rational analysis can play in helping us make moral choices among them. Where values are incommensurable, we find that there is "no compelling principle, or rational method, of balancing one value against another" (Hampshire 1983, 118–19). As such, incommensurability attests to what Joseph Raz has called "the indeterminacy of reason" or "the inability of reason to guide our action" in making such choices (1986, 333–34). It means, to use Hampshire's words, that "no sufficient reason of any kind is on occasion available to explain a decision made after careful reflection in a situation of moral conflict" and that "our divided, and comparatively open, nature requires one to choose, without sufficient reason, between irreconcilable dispositions and contrary claims" (Hampshire 1983, 118). To say that we must choose without "sufficient reason" is not to suggest, of course, that we cannot make these choices or, for that matter, that we cannot offer our reasons for our choices. Rather, it means simply that some of the reasons we might offer in support of making a particular choice are incommensurable with other reasons we might offer were we to make an alternative choice. In this sense, our choices among valued options may be quite reasoned, but they are, nevertheless, underdetermined by reason.

A classic example of incommensurability among values that is often pointed to is the incommensurability that exists between money and friendship (Raz 1986; Lukes 1989; Gray 2000). We all know that, in the course of our lives, there are instances where we may sacrifice money for friendship or vice versa, as when, for example, we are faced with a choice between either spending time at a job assignment or spending time with friends. However, while we often make such choices, the fact is that most of us would never consider paying other people money in return for their friendship or, for that matter, consider accepting money from them in return for our friendship. In this sense, while we are perfectly capable of choosing between money and friendship, we simply refuse to compare the value of these goods. Indeed, the explicit exchange of money for friendship would be seen as destructive of the whole notion of friendship, at least as most of us have come to understand it. As Raz puts it, "Only those who hold the view that friendship is neither better nor worse than money, but is simply not comparable to money or other commodities are *capable* of having friends. Similarly only those who would not even consider exchanges of money for friendship are capable of having friends" (1986, 352). In other words, in order to understand properly the nature of friendship, one must first understand that it is incommensurable with money or other goods. This type of incommensurability applies to other social relationships and practices as well, including marriage and parenthood. In such cases, incommensurabilities are necessary to the very meaning of these relationships and practices, at least as we have come to understand them. They make "possible the pursuits and relationships of which they are a constitutive part" (Raz 1986, 354).

Why Is There Conflict among Values?

Value pluralism entails, therefore, both value incompatibility and value incommensurability. It is the presence of both of these conditions that makes for genuine value conflict. Some might ask here why is it that our values or moral claims should ever come into conflict with each other in the first place? One answer to this question is simply that our values are not the product of any rational plan or design. Rather, they represent our attempts to abstract from or to put into words the habits of behavior that are associated with the various social practices in which we, as human beings, engage, or have engaged in the past, in going about the everyday business of living: practices of working, eating, playing, loving, procreating, dealing with our families, learning and teaching, keeping peace with our neighbors or fighting with them, praying with others to our various deities, dying, and so forth. As Michael Oakeshott once wrote, "Moral ideals are not, in the first place, the products of reflective thought, the verbal expressions of unrealized ideas, which are then translated (with varying degrees of accuracy) into human behaviour; they are the products of human behaviour, of human practical activity, to which reflective thought gives subsequent, partial and abstract expression in words" (1991, 479–80).

Consequently, in light of the diverse character of our practical activities, as well as of the various particular interests or needs that they serve, there is little reason why we should expect that the values that we might happen to derive from any one set of practices should somehow turn out to be in harmony with those we have derived from others. Indeed, some conflict among these different values would seem almost inevitable. Loyalty to our own children, for example, may well conflict with fairness if we are coaching a soccer team in which they happen to be playing. In this respect, "moral conflict is typically a matter of beliefs that have been acquired in the attempt to serve one good purpose getting in the way of beliefs that have been developed in the course of serving another good purpose" (Rorty 2007, 81).

Yet another reason that we might expect conflict among our values or moral ends is that, historically, groups of men and women have developed moralities or conceptions of the good, just as they have developed languages, as a way of defining their identities in contrast to those of others. In seeking to distinguish themselves from other groups in terms of their particular practices and associated moralities, groups have often defined themselves in oppositional terms, that is, not simply in terms of who they are, but also in terms of who they are not. Consequently, in thinking about our own values or moral claims, we frequently define what we are for in terms of what we are against. In other words, in matters of morality as in logic, "all determination is negation" (Hampshire 2000, 34). In fact, as Hampshire notes, "Most influential conceptions of the good have defined themselves as rejections of their rivals: for instance, some of the ideals of monasticism were a rejection of the splendors and hierarchies of the Church, and this rejection was part of the original sense and purpose of the monastic ideal. Some forms of fundamentalism, both Christian and others, define themselves as a principled rejection of secular, liberal, and permissive moralities" (34–35).

Moreover, this principle of "determination by negation" does not apply only to different religious sects. It applies also to the values of secular liberal communities where "the essence of liberal morality is the rejection of any final and exclusive authority, natural or supernatural, and of the accompanying compulsion and censorship. In this context, freedom itself is felt, and is cherished, as a nega-

tive notion: no walls of dogma, no unquestionable rules from priests and politicians: the future is to be an open field for discovery. Openness is a negative concept" (Hampshire 2000, 35).

Moral conflict is grounded, therefore, in the negative or oppositional character of different systems of morality in different groups, as well as the variety of
different social practices in which we engage. In this regard, it follows that value
pluralism, just like any other set of moral ideas or beliefs, turns out to be a product of our moral practices. That this should be so should not surprise us, and
it helps to explain why, although arguably always with us, value pluralism has
emerged as an especially important idea in the context of late modern societies
that contain diverse, and sometimes conflicting, communities and ways of life.
John Gray recognizes this when he argues that the idea that "the human good
is shown in rival ways of living" is "no longer only a claim in moral philosophy"
(2000, 34). Rather, it has also become "a fact of ethical life" (34). According to
Gray, "Today we know that human beings flourish in conflicting ways, not from
the detached standpoint of an ideal observer, but as a matter of common experience. As migration and communication have commingled ways of life that
used to be distinct and separate, the contention of values has become our common condition. For us, pluralism is an historical fate" (34). Richard Bellamy has
similarly observed how modernizing processes "have enhanced polyethnicity
and multiculturalism," and how today individuals must "juggle the conflicting
values of work, family, friends, locality, gender, ethnicity, religion and so on"
(2000, 198). In other words, as a result of our current condition of a diversity of
moral ends or conceptions of the good, the idea of value pluralism now forces
itself upon us, no longer simply as an intellectual abstraction or philosophical
puzzle, but rather also as a part of our ordinary lived experience. In this respect,
then, the idea of pluralism can be seen as "a response to the diversity of incommensurable values and perspectives that is a peculiarly prominent feature of
early post-modernity" (Gray 1993, ix).

Value Pluralism and Relativism

The idea of value pluralism, as described above, is sometimes seen as a form of
relativism, as an endorsement of the idea that in matters of morality "anything
goes" or that what we like to call morality is simply a matter of personal taste.
For this reason, value pluralism has, on occasion, been regarded with suspicion.
However, in my view, to equate value pluralism with relativism in this way is
simply to misunderstand what value pluralism really means. For one thing, there
seem to be at least some limits on what nearly all of us consider to be human

values. As Berlin reminds us, while it is perfectly true that our "ends [or] moral principles are many," at the same time, they are not "infinitely many" (1992, 11). For example, as he says, "if I find a man to whom it literally makes no difference whether he kicks a pebble or kills his family, since either would be a solution to *ennui* or inactivity, I shall not be disposed, like consistent relativists, to attribute to him merely a different code of morality from my own or that of most men, or declare that we disagree on essentials, but shall begin to speak of insanity or inhumanity; I shall be inclined to consider him mad, as a man who thinks he is Napoleon is mad" (Berlin 1979, 166).

In other words, when a man or a woman talks or acts in such a way that violates certain basic common norms or values, we have difficulty in continuing to think of them as fully human. Indeed, the very fact that we are able to communicate with other cultures across both time and place, the fact that we are able to recognize the inhabitants of such cultures as human beings somewhat like ourselves, rather than as something else entirely, provides us with phenomenological evidence that all human beings seem to share at least some common values. To use Berlin's words, then, "we are free to criticise the values of other cultures, to condemn them, but we cannot pretend not to understand them at all, or to regard them simply as subjective" (1992, 11). In this sense, there is a world of "objective values [or] ends that men pursue for their own sakes" (11). These values may be said to be objective, at least in the sense that we see the pursuit of such values as "part of what it is to be a human being" (Berlin 2000, 12).

Furthermore, while it is true that individuals and groups certainly can differ quite sharply in their conceptions of the good, it is also true that much greater agreement is likely to be found with respect to what constitute evils. Notwithstanding the very real moral differences that exist between us, there remains, for nearly all of us, what Hampshire calls the "great evils," the evils that are "truly perennial" (2000, xi). These include, for example, "the unchanged horrors of human life, the savage and obvious evils, which scarcely vary from culture to culture or from age to age: massacres, starvation, imprisonment, torture, death, and mutilation in war, tyranny and humiliation—in fact, the evening and the morning news. Whatever the divergences in conceptions of the good, these primary evils stay constant and undeniable as evils to be at all costs averted, or almost all costs" (43). These types of evils—unlike whatever visions of a better social order we might hold—are not dependent upon the particular culture in which we happen to have been brought up. Rather, they "are felt as evils directly and without recourse to the norms of any particular way of life or to any specific set of moral ideas" (xii). Such evils need not "be revealed and certified by argument as evil before they are felt as evil" (xii). They are "immediately felt as evils by any normally responsive person, unless she has perhaps been distracted from natural feeling by some theory that explains them away: for example, as necessary parts of God's design" (xii).

The Rejection of Monism

Value pluralism, therefore, does not mean that our values are merely a matter of personal opinion or taste. It does not mean, "I like my coffee with milk and you like it without; I am in favor of kindness and you prefer concentration camps" (Berlin 2000, 11). Rather, value pluralism asserts that we know—both from our experience and from history—that the values or moral claims that we have come to believe to be true often do conflict with one another in irreconcilable ways. To put it another way, value pluralism can be seen here as a refutation of the idea of monism. Monism is the age-old and seductive idea that, even though we may not always be able or willing to see it, even though we may lack sufficient intelligence or goodwill to recognize it right now, there is, in fact, an underlying harmony in human values such that any conflicts that might appear to exist among them can be resolved by appeal to some higher principle or standard. As Berlin argues, monism is the idea that "all truly good things are linked to one another in a single, perfect whole; or, at the very least cannot be incompatible with one another" and that "the realization of the pattern formed by them is the one true end of all rational activity, both public and private" (1969, x). It entails "the notion of the perfect whole, the ultimate solution, in which all good things coexist" (Berlin 1992, 13). Monism rests upon a belief that, in the final analysis, there is, as Hampshire explains, "a common basis, . . . a single reason behind all moral claims, . . . an ultimate harmony among moral claims" (1983, 118). This "ultimate solution" or "ultimate harmony" may differ, of course, depending upon the particular type or brand of monism that is advanced. For example, for some it may be some type of ultimate good against which all other values and actions can be evaluated, whereas for others it may be simply some common measure or medium such as utility in terms of which different values can be expressed. Alternatively, monism may consist in some canonical principle or set of principles that can provide for a hierarchical ranking of different values.

Monism, in its various forms, has exercised a powerful influence over a wide range of Western thought going back to Plato (Kekes 1993; Parekh 1996). It shows itself in Platonic, Christian, utilitarian, and deontological notions of the good. In fact, monism lies "at the very heart of traditional rationalism, religious and aesthetic, metaphysical and scientific, transcendental and naturalistic, that has been characteristic of western civilization" (Berlin 1982, 68). This is important because it means that, in rejecting monism, value pluralism then rejects much of what has been central to Western scholarly reflection about the nature of what is good.

The Case for Value Pluralism

If so much of our philosophical thinking has been monistic in character, then, the reader might reasonably ask at this point why it is that we should accept pluralism and reject monism. This question frankly is still subject to considerable controversy among philosophers (see, for example, Archard 1996). However, perhaps the most cogent answer is a phenomenological one that Berlin himself provides. This is that, from our own ordinary experience of the world, we know that our values often do conflict with one another in irreconcilable ways and that, in the absence of overwhelming evidence to the contrary, there seems little reason to reject the reality of this experience. As Berlin says,

> if we are not armed with an *a priori* guarantee of the proposition that a total harmony of true values is somewhere to be found, . . . we must fall back on the ordinary resources of empirical observation and ordinary human knowledge. And these certainly give us no warrant for supposing (or even understanding what would be meant by saying) that all good things, or all bad things for that matter, are reconcilable with each other. The world that we encounter in ordinary experience is one in which we are faced with choices between ends equally ultimate, and claims equally absolute, the realization of some of which must inevitably involve the sacrifice of others. (1969, 168)

Hampshire similarly notes here how "we ordinarily encounter serious moral problems as conflicts between moral claims which, considered *a priori,* seem absolute and exceptionless and which are in fact irreconcilable in the situations that present the problem" (1983, 115). According to him,

> we naturally think, when uncorrupted by theory, of a multiplicity of moral claims, which sometimes come into conflict with each other, just as we think of a multiplicity of human virtues, which sometimes come into conflict with each other; so much so, that if one hears that someone has a moral problem, one immediately assumes that he is confronted with just such a difficult conflict of claims. It is typical and essential, not marginal and accidental, that moral reasoning should be concerned with such conflicts. Unavoidable conflict of principles of conduct, and not a harmony of purposes, is the stuff of morality, as we ordinarily experience it. (116)

In other words, the monist view that all conflicts among the values that we think important to us are ultimately resolvable simply does not seem to fit well with our moral experience as human beings. In fact, a monist world, in which all values can be harmonized, is "a world altogether beyond our ken" (Berlin 1992, 13). The moral principles that would exist in this type of world are "not the principles with which, in our daily lives, we are acquainted" (13).

Especially revealing in this regard is the fact that, in a monist world, one in which there was a harmony of values, we would no longer be able to make sense of that feeling of loss or regret we so often feel when making difficult moral decisions. To be sure, even in a monist world, we might feel some apprehension or uncertainty in regard to whether or not a choice we had made was the correct one, whether or not we had perhaps made an error in selecting one value over another. Cases of buyer's remorse in moral choices would not be impossible even if monism were true. On the other hand, a true sense of loss would be simply out of place. After all, if there really were some common moral denominator or some *summum bonum*, in terms of which all conflicts among values could be resolved, then nothing really would be lost at all by giving up one value as long as we believed that more good was to be gained by securing another value. In such an idealized life, "nothing of value need ever be lost or sacrificed" (Berlin 1969, li). If, for example, as Kekes argues, we happened to follow a utilitarian calculus and "we thought that all values derived from whatever they contributed to happiness, then we would simply choose the value that gave more happiness, and we could not regret having forgone lesser happiness, since what we want is greater happiness" (1993, 57).

In short, what we lose in monist views of the world is, perhaps ironically, a sense of loss itself. This sense of loss, which we so often seem to experience in making moral choices, can become especially pronounced when we are forced to choose not so much among different goods but rather among different bads or evils. These are the sorts of dilemmas that arise when, as Raz puts it, each option "involves wrongdoing" and "whatever the agent does he will do wrong" (1986, 364). Gray provides an example of this type of choice from public administration. He cites the case of a British wartime minister who fired all of his typists because he knew that one of them was leaking secrets to the enemy, but he did not know which one. This minister honestly believed that he took the right action. Nonetheless, he felt a clear sense of loss in knowing that, whatever he chose to do, he would commit a wrong. He knew that the action he took would inflict "a lifelong injustice on all but one of the typists" and that it "contained irreparable wrong" (Gray 2000, 47). From the point of view of our moral experience, whether or not we might agree with the minister's actions, these feelings would seem perfectly understandable. Yet, if a monist perspective were to be taken seriously, this feeling of having committed a wrong would make no sense at all. It would reflect simply irrationality or confusion on the part of the minister.

To put this another way, a monist world would be one in which there would no longer be any genuine moral conflict. It would be a world in which, as Kekes describes it, "all conflicts among values [would] have a decisive resolution" (1993, 57). According to a monist viewpoint, what appeared to us initially as moral conflicts could arise only out of some defect or limitation in our character or in our understanding—some failure on our part to make the necessary connections between our own actions and the unitary good. A sense of moral conflict would be, as Lukes puts it, no more than a result of "ignorance or error, or of individual or social pathology" (1989, 127). It would be simply "an affliction to be overcome" (127).

It is clear, therefore, that accepting monism would require a radical shift in our ordinary notions of morality. Indeed, were we really to accept the idea that all conflicts among values could, in fact, be resolved in terms of an appeal to some overarching end, then moral choices, at least as we have come to understand them in our ordinary lives, would simply disappear. They would be replaced by what were essentially instrumental or technological choices. In a purely monist world, there would no longer be any choices about ends. There would be only choices about what were the best means to accomplish those ends. To use Berlin's words, once we accept a monist conception of value, "problems can be only of means, all soluble by technological methods" (1992, 15). Furthermore, with the disappearance of genuine moral conflict and moral choices from our lives, much of what we understand to be human would also disappear. If all choices become essentially instrumental and technological, then at some point in the future all of the choices that are currently made by men and women could be made—at least in principle—by a machine or a computer. In this respect, a monist world would be one in which "the inner life of man, the moral and spiritual and aesthetic imagination, no longer speaks at all" (15).

Monist theories of the good therefore present serious conceptual difficulties for our everyday notions about moral choice. In light of these difficulties, it is surely reasonable, then, to ask of ethical monists, as Bernard Williams does, "what authority is theoretical tidiness or simplicity supposed to have against the concerns which one actually finds important?" (1979, xvii). If we accept that a conflict exists between monism and our ordinary moral experience, why should we accept monism and reject the evidence of our experience? After all, any effort to persuade us of the reality of a particular monist creed would surely require an extraordinarily powerful argument and, especially when one considers what Kekes has termed the "historical failures of the numerous attempts to establish the compatibility and commensurability of values" (1993, 58), it is frankly far from obvious that any such argument exists. In other words, as Gray puts it, "why should we seek to displace this datum of experience at the behest of any ethical theory" when "it is not as if such theories were themselves especially compelling" (1996, 63)?

The Dangers of Monism

Moreover, not only does monism appear incoherent with our ordinary moral experience, it turns out that it can also be potentially dangerous to moral conduct itself. It is important to recall Oakeshott's words here that "every moral ideal is potentially an obsession" and "too often the excessive pursuit of one ideal leads to the exclusion of others, perhaps all others; in our eagerness to realize justice we come to forget charity, and a passion for righteousness has made many a man hard and merciless" (1991, 476). Berlin puts the issue perhaps even more pointedly when he warns us that "the possibility of a final solution—even if we forget the terrible sense that these words acquired in Hitler's day—turns out to be an illusion; and a very dangerous one. For if one really believes that such a solution is possible, then surely no cost would be too high to obtain it: to make mankind just and happy and creative and harmonious for ever—what could be too high a price to pay for that?" (1992, 15). In other words, monism or a belief in a single criterion of goodness or value can breed an extreme form of instrumental rationalism in which monist ends may be used to justify any means, however despicable. Indeed, the belief that "it is in principle possible to discover a harmonious pattern in which all values are reconciled, and that it is towards this unique goal that we must make" can lead not only to "absurdities in theory," but also to "barbarous consequences in practice" (Berlin 1969, lv–lvi).

In advancing these criticisms, Berlin was clearly thinking about the excesses of totalitarian Nazi and Marxist regimes of the twentieth century. However, we should not imagine that modern liberal regimes are somehow exempt from the pernicious effects of monism. Hampshire warns here, in particular, of the destructive effects of the utilitarian form of monism on moral conduct, commonly expressed in liberal cultures, where the monist good consists in the promotion of a maximum of human happiness. In his view, "the utilitarian habit of mind has brought with it a new abstract cruelty in politics, a dull, destructive political righteousness: mechanical, quantitative thinking, leaden loveless minds setting out their moral calculations in leaden abstract prose, and more civilized and more superstitious people destroyed because of enlightened calculations that have proved wrong" (Hampshire 1983, 85). With the American experience in Vietnam clearly in mind, Hampshire criticizes the utilitarian approach in government for "making rational calculation of consequences the sole foundation of public policies," thereby "favoring a new callousness in policy, a dullness in sensibility, and sometimes moral despair, at least in respect of public affairs" (95).

Moral Conflict in Public Life

The argument for value pluralism advanced here rests, then, on the incoherence of monism with our moral experience, as well as the potential dangers of monism. However, one may reasonably ask, while value pluralism may pose a philosophical problem for monist theories of ethics, just how serious a problem is it for public administration? After all, if conflicts among incommensurable ends are relatively rare, then, while they may make for a certain level of discomfort when they occur, they surely need not preoccupy us too much as public administration writers or practitioners. Unfortunately, there is no reason to believe that this is the case and very good reason to believe that, in fact, value conflicts pervade much of the experience of those who work in government and public administration.

Stephen Bailey, one of the few writers in administrative ethics who have specifically addressed this issue of moral conflict, wrote over four decades ago of "the morally ambivalent effect of all public policy" that arises because "an adequate response to any social evil contains the seeds of both predictable and unpredictable pathologies" (1964, 237). According to Bailey, "The bittersweet character of all public policy needs little further elaboration: welfare policies may mitigate hunger but promote parasitic dependence; vacationing in forests open for public recreation may destroy fish, wild life, and through carelessness in the handling of fire, the forests themselves. Unilateral international action may achieve immediate results at the cost of weakening international instruments of conflict resolution. Half a loaf *may* be worse than no loaf at all. It also may be better in the long run but worse in the short run—and vice versa" (237). Because of this type of moral conflict, "there is not a moral vice which cannot be made into a relative good by context. There is not a moral virtue which cannot in peculiar circumstances have patently evil results" (239).

More recently, Gray has provided a lucid account of the value conflicts that face public officials who are involved in urban planning. He observes how, for some citizens, "freedom to stroll and saunter, to enjoy public spaces in safety and to encounter strangers" are central among the "goods of city life," whereas, for others, these "amenities of living in cities may take second place to the role of cities as sites for the creation of wealth and employment, . . . as places where we work, while we live—or aspire to live—elsewhere" (2000, 103). Also, not only may citizens disagree among themselves as to what are the goods of city life; citizens may also harbor, within themselves, conflicting desires with regard to what they really want from their cities. According to Gray, "Individuals may value a form of city life in which they can shop and work near where they live. At the same time, they may value the low prices and range of goods available in out-of-town shopping malls and the high incomes made possible by long-distance commuting. The cost of small-town living may be high prices and limited choice. The cost of a form of life devoted to high incomes and consumer choice may be a hideous post-urban sprawl. No one trade-off among these conflicting interests is uniquely reasonable" (101).

Consequently, when putting together their planning recommendations, urban planners also face difficult moral choices among conflicting values. They "cannot overlook the fact that their decisions can spell life or death for communities. Failing to provide public transport to rural communities can trigger a flight to the cities on the part of new generations. Putting roads through the centres of cities can uproot long-established street communities. There is no escaping these choices. . . . City planners cannot avoid taking a view on the worth of the ways of life their decisions affect" (Gray 2000, 101).

Moreover, value conflict involves more than the strategic choices among different public policies made by politicians and planners. It also affects the ordinary day-to-day decisions of public administrators as they seek to carry out these policies. Hendrik Wagenaar writes how, in public administration, "public programs are structured in such a way that they regularly confront the administrator with difficult value choices," so that "resolving value conflict is an intrinsic part of administrative life" (1999, 444). Telling a somewhat poignant story about the moral difficulties faced by a government physician who was charged with evaluating the disability claims of patients seeking government assistance, Wagenaar notes here that, because values and value conflict permeate public programs "straight into their most minute technical rulings, . . . the upshot is that administrators in the course of their everyday work, face thousands of large and small moral choices" (1999, 444–45).

Furthermore, not only are many of the values pursued by public officials incompatible with one another, it turns out that they are also often incommensurable with one another. William Galston acknowledges this fact in reflecting on his professional experience while working as a White House domestic policy advisor under President Clinton. He recalls how "over and over again I had the same experience: I would be chairing an interagency task force designed to reach a unified administration position on some legislative or regulatory proposal. As the representatives of the various departments argued for their various views, I found it impossible to dismiss any one of them as irrelevant to the decision, or as wholly lacking in weight. Nor could I reduce the competing considerations to a common measure of value; so far as I or anyone else could tell, they were irreducibly heterogeneous" (2002, 7).

The value conflicts that those in government must deal with are often especially difficult because these conflicts present them with moral dilemmas that entail choices not between actions that are morally desirable, but rather between actions that are morally disagreeable. These are the choices that give rise to Machiavelli's problem of "dirty hands," in which a ruler or government official "must choose between two courses of action both of which it would be wrong for him to undertake" (Walzer 1973, 160). Max Weber explicitly recognized this problem of dirty hands in politics when he argued, "No ethics in the world can dodge the fact that in numerous instances the attainment of 'good' ends is bound to the fact that one must be willing to pay the price of using morally dubious means" (1946, 121). This problem of choosing between morally disagreeable actions is often associated, especially nowadays, with extreme cases such as whether or not we ought to torture terrorists in order to obtain valuable information that could somehow save hundreds or thousands of lives. However, the problem also exists in the more seemingly mundane activities of public administrators; as Udo Pesch has pointed out, "the daily practice of the administrator appears to be overflowing with situations that give rise to the problem of . . . dirty hands" (2005, 165). These dilemmas are often faced, for example, by street-level public administrators, such as social workers, in their ordinary day-to-day dealings with citizens, where, as Steven Maynard-Moody and Michael Musheno have vividly documented, "the needs of individual citizen-clients exist in tension with the demands and limitations of rules" (2003, 93).

Moreover, as Michael Walzer has argued, "the dilemma of dirty hands is a central feature of political life" that arises "systematically and frequently" (1973, 162). This is because "the successful politician becomes the visible architect of our restraint" (163). He or she is the person who "taxes us, licenses us, forbids and permits us, directs us to this or that greater goal—all for our greater good," the person who "takes chances for our greater good that put us, or some of us, in danger," and who "uses violence and the threat of violence . . . against us," all of this "ostensibly for our greater good" (163). If this is true, then, as Hampshire observes, those who wield governmental power "should at all times be prepared for the occurrence of uncontrolled conflict of duties in situations which seem to exclude the possibility of a decent outcome, and in which all lines of action seem dishonourable or blameworthy" (1989, 170). It follows that those who choose to involve themselves in government and who wish to act morally must, in fact, abandon hope of moral innocence and learn to live with "the idea of guilty knowledge, of the expectation of unavoidable squalor and imperfection, of necessary disappointments and mixed results, of half success and half failure" (170).

The dilemma of "dirty hands" occurs in moral choices in everyday life, but it can create a particular problem for those who happen to work in government. This is because, on the one hand, "the assumption of a political role, and of power to change men's lives on a large scale" often requires "a withholding of some of the scruples that in private life would prohibit one from using people as a means to an end and also from using force and deceit" (Hampshire 1983, 123–24). We neither expect nor want our government leaders to act like moral saints because to have them do so would be to rob them of the power to satisfy our desires and hopes. It is for this reason, as Williams so aptly puts the matter, "sackcloth is not suitable dress for politicians, least of all successful ones" (1978, 64). On the other hand, there are real dangers when we seek to rationalize actions that are morally questionable. As Williams reminds us, "only those who are reluctant or disinclined to do the morally disagreeable when it is really necessary have much chance of not doing it when it is not necessary" (64). What is required on the part of those who work in government is "reluctance in the necessary case," by which he means "not just initial hesitation in reaching for the answer, but genuine disquiet when one arrives at it, . . . a sensibility to moral costs" (65). In other words, while we may not want our public officials to jeopardize the public good by being morally fastidious about the acts they take in the pursuit of important public objectives or values, neither do we want them to abandon all of their moral scruples and to be morally indifferent in regard to their own actions.

The fact that most of us can understand and appreciate perfectly well these types of dilemmas of dirty hands in government action provides further evidence of the incommensurability of moral claims in government and further refutation of any monist conception of the good. In a truly monist world, there would be no room for any such moral ambivalence concerning government actions. A particular government action would be determined either to promote or not to promote the overriding single good and, once this was decided, any further deliberation, whether external or internal, would be unnecessary and wasteful. In a utilitarian world, for example, suppose a local government were considering options for economic development and it had determined that the demolition of an older neighborhood and the involuntary seizure of the property of some of its residents was necessary so as to make way for new high-priced condominiums and upscale retail outlets. Suppose, furthermore, that this government had determined that this action would, in fact, promote the greatest happiness of the greatest number for the community it served. Given this situation, government officials taking such action could never be accused of having done any wrong or of having dirty hands. When we adopt this type of monist perspective, as Lukes succinctly puts it, "the problem of dirty hands . . . cannot exist" because "apparently dirty hands are clean" (1989, 131).

Conclusion

Notwithstanding the claims for monism that have been made since ancient times by many philosophers—not to mention also religious leaders—value pluralism is, then, at least for most of us, an empirical truth, not only in our choices in our private lives, but also in our choices in public life. Without value pluralism, whether as private citizens or government officials, we could make little or no sense of the moral conflicts that we often experience, of our feelings of regret or of dirty hands for some of the actions we have taken in life, or even of morality itself. As Hampshire puts it, "morality and conflict are inseparable" so that, without the notion of conflict, "the subject matter of morality is misrepresented and disappears from view" (1983, 1).

Despite the arguments for value pluralism advanced here, some may still worry that, in rejecting any overriding conceptions of the good, value pluralism means that moral choices among actions that promote incompatible and incommensurable ends must inevitably be arbitrary and that one choice is just as good as any other choice. Berlin himself certainly did not believe this to be the case, and he offered what may be some useful advice. He argued that, when facing choices among conflicting values, we should make such choices or judgments in light of the overall pattern of our values. We should "decide in the light of the general ideals, the overall pattern of life pursued by a man or a group or a society" (1969, l). Furthermore, we must be willing to make compromises. Collisions of values, "even if they cannot be avoided, can be softened" (Berlin 1992, 17). "Claims can be balanced, compromises can be reached . . . so much liberty and so much equality; so much for sharp moral condemnation, and so much for understanding a given human situation; so much for the full force of the law, and so much for the prerogative of mercy; for feeding the hungry, clothing the naked, healing the sick, sheltering the homeless. Priorities, never final and absolute, must be established" (17).

In such a decision-making process, "rules, values, principles must yield to each other in varying degrees in specific situations" (Berlin 1992, 17). In other words, the specific practical context in which values are found to be in conflict with one another must always be considered. "The best that can be done, as a general rule," according to Berlin, "is to maintain a precarious equilibrium that will prevent the occurrence of desperate situations, of intolerable choices"

(17–18). However, this will always be "an uneasy equilibrium, which is constantly threatened and in constant need of repair" (19). Berlin's words here strongly suggest the essentially political character of the way in which societies should deal with conflicts among different values or conceptions of the good. In light of this, it is helpful to turn next to an examination of the idea and practice of politics and the crucial role that politics plays in different societies in assisting them in the management of value conflicts.

3
Politics, Conciliation, and Value Pluralism

In the previous chapter, it was argued that conflicts arise among incompatible and incommensurable values or conceptions of the good not just within individuals, but also within societies or communities. This chapter will examine how the practice of politics helps societies and communities in dealing with such conflicts. I argue here that politics can help protect and foster value pluralism by expanding the range of values that are taken into account in formulating and administering public policies and programs and, also, by limiting the application of coercive power by government. Before beginning this examination, however, we need to understand better what we mean by the term *politics*. *Politics,* after all, is a rather ambiguous term and, as such, subject to a variety of different interpretations. As Kenneth Minogue warns us, "as a theatre of illusion, politics does not reveal its meanings to the careless eye" (1995, 6). Critical theorists and feminists, for example, nowadays often seek to expand the meaning of what is political so far as to encompass every aspect of our lives and relationships, an idea perhaps best captured in the slogan "the personal is political." However, Bernard Crick probably captures its meaning best—at least within the context of our Anglo-American and European traditions of thinking and practice— when he argues that politics should be understood as a manner of governance in which whoever happens to rule a society, be it a monarch, an elected assembly, or some other body, attempts to reconcile the different interests and values that exist within that society by using methods of conciliation and compromise rather than force. Politics, when seen in this fashion, is, as noted earlier, "a way of ruling in divided societies without undue violence" (Crick [1962] 1993, 141). It is a practical response to the problem of "preserving a community" that has simply "grown too complicated for either tradition alone or pure arbitrary rule to preserve it without the undue use of coercion" (24).

Crick's conception of politics here presupposes two conditions for the practice of politics: first, that there exists a complex pluralistic type of society in which there has emerged a diversity of interests and different values and, second, that there is a shared desire within that society to avoid the use of violence in settling these differences. As Crick puts it, to view politics in this way "is to assert, historically, that there are some societies at least which contain a variety of different interests and differing moral viewpoints and [also] to assert, ethically, that conciliation is at least to be preferred to coercion among normal people" (1993, 141). If we are to understand better how politics affects the process of governance and, more specifically, how it helps to resolve conflicts among values or moral ends, it is helpful to begin by examining each of these two conditions in more depth.

Politics and Political Pluralism

For Crick, politics arises where there is "a variety of different interests and moral ends which must be reconciled" (1993, 133). It rests on "an empirical generalization and on an ethical commitment: that there is diversity" and that such diversity "is normally good" (170). Viewed from this perspective, politics can never be about the imposition of any single truth or any single set of truths on society. As Crick bluntly puts it, "we cannot through politics grasp for an absolute ideal" (15). Rather, politics "represents at least some tolerance of differing truths, some recognition that government is possible, indeed best conducted, amid the open canvassing of rival interests" (18). It "arises from the fact and apperception of diversity, not from any ideal or material drive towards complete unity" (172), and it rests on a presumption that such "diversity is better than unity" (160). Indeed, politics is to be desired because it "enables us to enjoy variety without suffering anarchy or the tyranny of single truths" (26). Politics entails, therefore, not only the existence of a diversity of interests and values but also the acceptance or toleration of such diversity.

Seen in this fashion, the practice of politics does not require what David Easton, a prominent American political scientist, once famously termed an "authoritative allocation of values for a society" (1953, 129) or "authoritative social decisions about how goods, both spiritual and material, are to be distributed" (135). Indeed, there would be arguably no politics at all if there ever were "a single authoritative source for the allocation of all values and for the determination of all policies" or some "final and lasting absolute allocation of resources and values" (Crick 1993, 171). Politics here is not about anything nearly as grandiose as the allocating of values for an entire society. Rather, it is simply "that type of government where politics proves successful in ensuring reasonable stability and order" (21).

In short, therefore, to engage in politics as such does not seem to require much, if any, consistency or agreement among different individuals and groups in a community about the ends, objectives, or values that ought to be pursued by that community. As Crick notes, if there were "a natural unanimity of opinion in any society on all great issues, . . . politics would, indeed, be unnecessary" (Crick 1993, 64). The only consensus that the practice of politics really requires is simply a willingness to resolve differences among individuals and groups using politics rather than force or what Crick terms "a pragmatic agreement . . . to do things politically" (176). What holds groups together in a political order is nothing more than "a common interest in sheer survival" and the fact that "they practice politics—not [that] they agree about 'fundamentals'" (24). The common good in politics lies only in "the process of practical reconciliation" of different interests and values, not in "some allegedly objective 'general will' or 'public interest'" (24).

In this respect, we should take care not to conflate politics with other related ideas about governance such as democracy. American public administration, of course, has long been concerned with the idea of democracy and, indeed, our field arguably emerged out of a question about how to reconcile an efficient and energetic public administration with the values of a democratic state. However, while a reasonable argument may be made that, in many modern societies such as ours, democracy has become characteristic of the practice of politics, at the same time, democracy on its own can sound the death knell of politics. As Crick observes, "democracy as a social movement must exist in nearly all modern forms of political rule," but, "taken alone and as a matter of principle, it is the destruction of politics" (1993, 56). The problem that democracy poses for politics here lies in the democratic notion of popular sovereignty, which, if unfettered, makes the practice of politics impossible. Indeed, this notion of "the sovereignty of the people, . . . if taken too seriously is an actual step towards totalitarianism" because "it allows no refuge and no contradiction, no private apathy even" (60). As such, the notion of popular sovereignty is "un- or even apolitical" (61). When the phrase "sovereignty of the people" is used as a constant justification for whatever coercion or force a government might wish to employ against individuals and groups in society, then clearly it is no longer a justification for politics, as Crick understands the term, but rather simply an excuse for the suspension of politics altogether. As Crick puts it, "the democratic doctrine of the sovereignty of the people . . . threatens, then, the essential perception that all known advanced societies are pluralistic and diverse, which is the seed and the root of politics" (62).

This idea that politics entails a diversity of interests and values is no mere invention of Crick. To the contrary, it was Aristotle who expressed such an idea early on in the tradition of Western political discourse when, in critiquing Plato, he wrote that since "good is spoken of in as many ways as being [is spoken of], . . . the good cannot be some common and single universal" (1999, 1.6.3). From Aristotle's perspective, the good could never be "something common corresponding to a single idea" (1:6:11). With regard to politics, Aristotle recognized that a state governed in a political fashion, or what he termed a "polis," should be one composed not only of "a *number* of men," but also of "different *kinds* of men" (1946, 2.2.3). Accordingly, he argued that, in seeking a unified polis, we should be careful not to sacrifice the diversity that makes a polis possible. As Aristotle saw it, "there is a point at which a polis, by advancing in unity, may cease to be a polis: there is another point, short of that, at which it may still remain a polis, but will none the less come near to losing its essence, and will thus be a worse polis. It is as if you were to turn harmony into mere unison, or to reduce a theme to a single beat" (1946, 2.5.14).

Drawing on this Aristotelian tradition of thought, Hannah Arendt has argued that "the reality of the public realm relies on the simultaneous presence of innumerable perspectives and aspects in which the common world presents itself and for which no common measurement or denominator can ever be devised" (2000, 204). As she puts it, "though the common world is the common meeting ground of all, those who are present have different locations in it, and the location of one can no more coincide with the location of another than the location of two objects. Being seen and being heard by others derive their significance from the fact that everybody sees and hears from a different position. This is the meaning of public life" (204).

More recently, Hanna Pitkin, also drawing upon Aristotle, observes similarly that political life is characterized by "the problem of *creating* unity, in a context of diversity, rival claims, unequal power, and conflicting interests" (1993, 215). As she notes, "in the absence of rival claims and conflicting interests, a topic never enters the political realm. But for the political collectivity, the 'we' to act, those conflicting claims and interests must be resolved in a way that continues to preserve the collectivity" (215). Viewed in this way, politics involves a "kind of simultaneous awareness of innumerable perspectives on a shared public enterprise" (217).

Sheldon Wolin argues likewise that the "basic dilemma of political judgments" is "how to create a common rule in a context of differences" (1960, 61).

Politics, in Wolin's view, involves "concessions and modifications in a policy" (62). This is not simply because "it is a good thing to formulate policies that will reflect a sensitivity to variations and differences throughout the society, but rather that a political society is simultaneously trying to act and to remain a community" (62). For Wolin, "a truly political art" is one that is "framed to deal with conflict and antagonism" (43), and political judgment must involve assessing "conflicting claims, all of which possess a certain validity" (63).

Furthermore, the idea that politics is concerned with the reconciliation of a diversity of different interests and values and that we cannot and should not, in Aristotle's words, "reduce a theme to a single beat" is one that has formed an important part of our traditional Anglo-American constitutional thinking going back to the early eighteenth century. For example, John Trenchard and Thomas Gordon, two prominent English radical Whigs, known collectively as Cato, whose writings were widely read by the American colonists, observed that "a diversity in speculations is so far from clogging the publick good, that it evidently promotes the same" and that "to attempt to reduce all men to one standard of thinking is absurd in philosophy, impious in religion, and faction in a state" (1995, 276). They believed that "the power and sovereignty of magistrates" should be "so divided into different channels and committed to the power of so many different men, with different interests and views, that the majority of them could seldom or never find their account in betraying their trust in fundamental instances" (417).

Later in the eighteenth century, James Madison recognized the inevitability of a diversity of interests and values in politics when, in discussing the problem of political faction, he wrote that it was "impracticable" to expect that every citizen would have "the same opinions, the same passions, and the same interests" (Wills 1982, 43). This was because, "as long as the reason of man continues fallible, and he is at liberty to exercise it, different opinions will be formed" (43). As Madison noted, "when men exercise their reason coolly and freely, on a variety of distinct questions, they inevitably fall into different opinions" (260). Indeed, from Madison's perspective, a diversity of different camps of opinion was itself a sign of freedom. While wary of factionalism, in considering the idea of a nation "free from parties," he observed that an "extinction of parties necessarily implies either a universal alarm for the public safety, or an absolute extinction of liberty" (260–61).

Seeming to echo Trenchard and Gordon, Madison's solution to the problem of faction was to attempt to create an extended republic in which he believed there would be such a great diversity of interests and opinions that it would be difficult for any one group of citizens to impose their will by force upon the rest. Free government, according to Madison, would be secured by a "multiplicity of interests" and a "multiplicity of sects" (Wills 1982, 264). As Madison put it, "Extend the sphere, and you take in a greater variety of parties and interests; you make it less probable that a majority of the whole will have a common motive to invade the rights of other citizens; or if such a common motive exists, it will be more difficult for all who feel it to discover their own strength, and to act in unison with each other" (48). Thus for Madison, "divide et impera," or "divide and rule," while a "reprobated axiom of tyranny," was also "under certain qualifications, the only policy by which a republic can be administered on just principles" (Kammen 1986, 73). Pluralism was to be used to restrain the tyranny of the majority because a majority faction, if allowed to dominate government, would, as Madison saw it, "sacrifice to its ruling passion or interest, both the public good and the rights of other citizens" (Wills 1982, 45).

In other words, as Arendt points out, the idea of "the people" never "became a singular" for the founders (2000, 271). Rather, "the American concept of people" was "identified with a multitude of voices and interests" so that "the word 'people' retained for them the meaning of manyness, of the endless variety of a multitude whose majesty resided in its very plurality" (271). It is for this reason that the founders were opposed to any notion of public opinion understood as a "potential unanimity of all" and why "they never referred to public opinion in their argument, as Robespierre and the men of the French Revolution invariably did to add force to their own opinions; in their eyes, the rule of public opinion was a form of tyranny" (271).

Politics and the Avoidance of Coercion

In addition to this idea of political pluralism, the view of politics advanced here also presumes a distinct preference for the use of conciliation and negotiation and an aversion to the use of force in settling disputes among individuals and groups. Politics is seen, in this manner, as a form of governing a state that is distinguished from, rather than inclusive of, the use of violence and coercion. It is about the conciliation of different groups, and it emerges whenever a ruler or ruling group finds that the use of coercion and violence that is required to govern has become either impossible or, at the very least, unpalatable or too costly. In this respect politics arises, therefore, because of what are seen by rulers as the limits of coercive power. As such, politics entails what Crick terms "a recognition of restraints" that "may be moral, but more often . . . is simply prudential" (1993, 21). Viewed in this way, politics is "a product of being unable, without more violence and risk than one can stomach, to govern alone" (21). It involves a realization of the "incalculability of violence," a recognition that, while "it is, of course, often possible to rule alone, . . . it is always highly difficult and highly dangerous" (21). As such, far from including coercion, politics is "motivated . . . in a dislike of coercion" (32).

Some might object here to the exclusion of coercion or force from the definition of politics. Easton, for example, argues that while "we are accustomed to associate the mechanisms for deciding political issues with peaceful, even perhaps rational, procedures, . . . there is no prior reason why this must be the case" and "violence itself is a recognized, even though usually a deplored, procedure for arriving at authoritative policy" (1953, 141). From his perspective, violence is "as much a part of the political process as peaceful means" (141). Of course, social scientists should be perfectly free to define terms in whatever fashion they find useful. However, such a broad definition of politics would seem frankly rather odd in that it just does not fit very well with our ordinary understanding of the term. Such a view of politics veers too far from what we normally mean when we say of a person that he or she is acting in a "political" fashion. As Crick points out, "when ordinary people talk of someone 'being political,' they do not mean that he is either administering or making (or acting in response to) a command" (1993, 169).

All of this, of course, is not to make the naive claim that there is never any need for the use of coercion or force on the part of government, even when government is practiced in a properly political fashion. To the contrary, as Crick himself concedes, under certain conditions, "political systems may need to suspend political rule and may survive such periods of suspension" (1993, 179). Conciliation "is better than violence—but it is not always possible" (160). Indeed, following the view of Hobbes, Crick regards the ability of government to exercise coercive power, when required to keep order, as a necessary condition for the practice of political rule. According to him, "the fact of government must exist, both historically and logically, [prior to] politics" (178). Politics in idea and practice "presumes that order already exists, both as a historical condition and as a potential . . . to be reasserted in times of emergency" (178). This is because "politics, to be a stable and possible method of rule, requires some settled order" (28). In other words, while politics is about the use of conciliation by government, rather than the use of coercion, at the same time politics can exist only where government is seen as having the capacity to keep order, and this in turn requires that the use of such coercion by government is always a possible option even though it is not a preferred option. The use of coercion or force by government, while not a part of politics itself, is, as it were, waiting in the wings should politics fail to reconcile peacefully differences in interests and values among different individuals and groups in society. Nonetheless, as Crick argues, in a political regime "political rule is the most preferable type of government in any but times of desperate emergency" (172). As he puts it, "conciliation is more part of the human condition than the violence which is necessary to achieve unity," and we should "keep violence and coercion as a final and exceptional reserve to defend the state itself" (172).

Crick's notion here that politics arises from a desire to settle differences by conciliation rather than force appears to fit well with our own understanding of how the practice of politics has actually emerged in Western political history rather than in political theory. Gianfranco Poggi, for example, has described the emergence in Europe of the medieval "ständestaat," or "polity of the estates," out of the practices of monarchs consulting with the various estates of their realms, including the nobility, the clergy, and the towns. Poggi observes how, within these states, "both the normal exercise and the occasional reassertion of rights (even rights of rule) became less rough-and-ready, less openly coercive and threatening to the security of order, more literate and legalistic. Much political business now involved taking and giving advice prior to giving and enforcing commands; consulting interested parties, official documents, and qualified authorities; and reaching decisions, or voicing objections to or reservations about decisions, on stated grounds" (1978, 57). Poggi concedes that these "largely novel modalities of the political process" were "often brutally interrupted by straightforward aggression, usurpation, or repression," but, at the same time, he argues that "we can see prefigured [in them] the predominantly discursive, businesslike temper of the internal political processes of the modern state" (57).

Poggi's analysis comports well with Joseph Strayer's short but nevertheless insightful examination of the emergence of the medieval state in Europe. According to Strayer, within the medieval state "consent was required for all acts of government, either explicit consent in the form of a grant by subjects or implicit consent to the acts of a court. This emphasis on consent was not just theory. . . . It was an inescapable political fact. No state had the military power, the bureaucratic personnel, or even the information needed to impose unpopular measures on opposition groups that had any political and social standing. The cooperation of local leaders was essential for implementing any administrative decision" (1970, 61).

Minogue, in a similar vein, sees the political institution of parliaments specifically as arising historically out of the inability of monarchs to rule alone. According to him,

> the essence of medieval politics lay in the fact that the king could not rule—even to the extent of carrying out the very limited functions of rule as it was understood at that time—without the cooperation of partners. He had to consult the nobles, the magnates of the Church, and, in time, representatives from the towns who could make commitments of

money. It was this situation which generated the quite new institution of parliaments. . . . Kings needed parliaments to agree [to] taxation and sometimes to give weight to royal policy in international dealings. Subjects valued them as they offered an opportunity to influence the law and to secure remedies against the abuse of power. (1995, 29–30)

G. M. Trevelyan states the matter in his characteristically Whiggish fashion when he describes how, in England, Parliament "had no one man for its maker" but rather was "the natural outcome, through long centuries, of the common sense and the good nature of the English people, who have usually preferred committees to dictators, elections to street fighting, and 'talking shops' to revolutionary tribunals" (1959, 152). As he notes, Parliament, in medieval times, "grew up gradually as a convenient means of smoothing out differences and adjusting common action between powers who respected one another" (152). According to Trevelyan, "the English people have always been distinguished for their 'Committee sense,' their desire to sit round and talk till an agreement or compromise is reached," and it was this "national peculiarity" that was "the true origin of the English Parliament" (152–53). Finally, Barrington Moore, while taking a clearly far less romantic view of English history than Trevelyan, one that emphasizes its "violent past," observes nonetheless how in England "the fact that Parliament existed meant that there was a flexible institution which constituted both an arena into which new social elements could be drawn as their demands arose and an institutional mechanism for settling peacefully conflicts among these groups" (1993, 29). This, along with the "absence of any strong apparatus of repression" that was available to the ruling groups to suppress political agitation, contributed during the nineteenth century, in his view, to "England's progress toward democracy" (39).

All of this indicates that the idea of a preference for conciliation over force is integral to our own historical understanding of the idea and practice of politics. Moreover, it can be argued that this preference for conciliation over force is implicit in the very design of the Constitution of the United States. Indeed, Bernard Bailyn has argued that "tension, balance, adversarial clashes leading to conciliating moderation lay at the core of the *Federalist* writers' thought" (2003, 123). Madison deliberately sought to implant politics into the separation of powers between different branches of government by making sure that "those who administer each department" had "the necessary constitutional means, and personal motives, to resist encroachments of the others" so that ambition could "be made to counteract ambition" (Wills 1982, 262). Madison's aim in separating power was "to divide and arrange the several offices in such a manner as that each may be a check on the other" (263). Moreover, as already noted above, in providing for an extended federal republic, Madison also hoped that "among the great variety of interests, parties, and sects which it embraces, a coalition of a majority of the whole society could seldom take place on any other principles than those of justice and the general good" (265). Through these types of constitutional institutions, Madison, as well as the other founders, sought what were essentially a series of veto points that would help limit the ability of any one group within government to impose its will by force upon others and that would encourage groups, as they sought their own particular ends through government, to accommodate themselves by means of politics to others seeking different ends.

Robert Dahl recognized the tendency of our constitutional checks and balances to encourage conciliation when, despite his sharp criticisms of Madison's constitutional ideas, he argued that Madison's constitutional system did, in fact, help to encourage the development of a "markedly decentralized system" of government in which "decisions are made by endless bargaining; perhaps in no other national political system is bargaining so basic a component of the political process" (1956, 150). More recently, Timothy O'Neill argues that "the Founders relied on incentives for cooperation to form a government capable of achieving the proper ends of government, not on checks that would lock the system in an unhelpful stalemate" (1988, 372). The founders hoped that "political checks driven by political ambitions would restrain the misuse of power while rewarding opportunities for cooperation among the members of the government" (385). What they sought through checking the misuse of power, according to O'Neill, was "a republic of politics, not laws" (385).

Finally, in order to see just how widely accepted this notion of politics as conciliation and compromise has been, it is perhaps worth noting that it was one of the Constitution's leading opponents who articulated most clearly the idea that conciliation is preferable to force in government. According to the Federal Farmer,

> In viewing the various governments instituted by mankind, we see their whole force reducible to two principles—the important springs which alone move the machines, and give them their intended influence and controul, are force and persuasion: by the former men are compelled, by the latter they are drawn. We denominate a government despotic or free, as the one or other principle prevails in it. . . . In despotic governments, one man, or a few men, independant of the people, generally make the laws, command obedience, and inforce it by the sword. . . . In free governments, the people, or their representatives, make the laws; their execution is principally the effect of voluntary consent and aid. . . . Our true object is to

give full efficacy to one principle, to arm persuasion on every side, and to render force as little necessary as possible. (Storing 1985, 73)

Politics and Freedom

A preference for conciliation over coercion, therefore, is part and parcel of our historical understanding and practice of politics. In light of this, it should not be surprising that there is a relationship between politics and what we have come to understand as freedom. According to Crick, "some freedom, at least, must exist wherever there is political rule" because "politics is a process of discussion, and discussion demands, in the original Greek sense, dialectic" (1993, 33). As he puts it, "Where there is politics there is freedom. There is some freedom, even if limited to contesting aristocratic clans, wherever government recognizes by institutional means the need to consult with conflicting interests on some regular and known basis—whether . . . through prudence (being unable to predict the outcome of coercion) or through principle (when, in some sense, the equal freedom of individuals or of other groups is part of the moral culture)" (184). Politics is "a preoccupation of free men, and its existence is a test of freedom" (140).

In other words, once politics rather than coercion is adopted as the primary means for dealing with the differences in interests and values that exist within a state, then the practice of politics by its very nature requires that representatives of at least some groups be permitted, at a minimum, to speak their minds openly and, where necessary, to voice their opposition to the wishes of a ruler or ruling group. It requires that individuals or groups be recognized as having, in a real sense, certain rights to defend their particular interests and values. Without this type of freedom, consultation will come to be seen as meaningless by all participants and the practice of politics will become impossible. This freedom, in turn, requires a recognition by the government and the groups with which it consults of some distinction between what is a public matter for government and what is a private matter for particular groups. Indeed, it is through the practice of politics that such a distinction between what is public or private is negotiated and preserved by such groups. As Crick writes, freedom is "neither isolation nor loneliness: it is the privacy of men who are committed to, even if not personally participating in, public politics," and "freedom and privacy both thrive when government is conducted publicly in the manner called political" (1993, 185). From this perspective, "freedom depends both on some distinction and on some *interplay* between private and public actions" (185). The idea and practice of freedom emerges, therefore, not, as some libertarians might claim, in the absence of government or in some Lockean state of nature or, for that matter, in some Rawlsian "original state," but rather in both the presence of government and the actions of groups and their representatives seeking to protect their interests and values in their negotiations with government. Even what we think of as a private sphere, as Richard Bellamy and Dario Castiglione argue, "is not a pre- or extra-political fact, but something that is achieved through politics" (1997, 598). In this respect, the protection of freedom can be seen as requiring engagement by citizens in politics because, as Crick notes, "people who use their liberty to avoid political life are more often done down than left in peace" (1993, 215). Engagement in politics is necessary to preserve freedom because "governments rarely leave people alone or treat justly those who will not stand up for themselves and combine politically" (216).

Politics creates freedom because it entails a respect for the idea of individual autonomy. It "presumes the existence of active and self-reliant individuals" (Crick 1993, 167). Politics, as Crick claims, presumes "some concern with personal identity—its assertion and its preservation" (49), and it must "respect individuality, rather than try to dissolve it away" (127). Indeed, it is the nature of political rule that, while it requires the involvement of citizens in political activity, it should not mandate such involvement against their wishes. As Crick argues, "a political régime cannot insist upon its citizens . . . asserting themselves in the public realm," and "it will not be a political régime at all if it tries to deny their spirited right to live inside their own privacy or outside in the public realm, as they choose" (54).

Lest Crick's idea that politics allows for the emergence of freedom be thought eccentric here, it is interesting to note that such an idea was, in fact, well understood by Machiavelli. In his accounts of the politics of ancient Rome, Machiavelli observed, for example, how "the disunion of the Senate and the people" had rendered "the republic of Rome powerful and free" (1950, 118). According to Machiavelli, "good laws . . . spring from those very agitations which have been so inconsiderately condemned by many" (120). Such political agitations, in his view, had "neither caused exiles nor any violence prejudicial to the general good," but rather had "given rise to laws that were to the advantage of public liberty" (120). Consequently, as Machiavelli saw it, "every free state ought to afford the people the opportunity of giving vent, to say, of their ambition" because "the demands of free people are rarely pernicious to their liberties" but, instead, "are generally inspired by oppressions, experienced or apprehended" (120).

This idea that politics allows for the expression of freedom is also related to Michel Foucault's argument that the exercise of power, as opposed to simple domination by force, presumes that those who are subject to power are capable of resisting it. According to Foucault, "in power relations there is necessarily the possibility of resistance because if there were no possibility of resistance (of violent resistance, flight, deception, strategies capable of reversing the situation) there would be no power relations at all" (2000a, 292). As Foucault argues, therefore "for power relations to come into play, there must be at least a certain degree of freedom on both sides" (292). In this respect, power relations are different from "states of domination" in that they can be understood "as strategic games between liberties—in which some try to control the conduct of others, who in turn try to avoid allowing their conduct to be controlled or try to control the conduct of the others" (299). Politics can be seen, then, as arising when, because of potential resistance, rulers find it necessary or prudent to engage in relationships of power with their subjects rather than dominate them by force, and, in doing so, politics facilitates the exercise of freedom.

Politics and Value Pluralism

Politics, as we have come to understand it, therefore involves a recognition, as well as an appreciation, of a diversity or multiplicity of interests and values among different groups in society and a preference for using conciliation rather than force in resolving differences among these groups, out of which emerges a concern with the protection of freedom. Crick's argument here is concerned simply with explicating and defending the idea and practice of politics and not with expounding any particular moral philosophy, albeit a monistic or a pluralistic one. Nonetheless, his argument intimates strongly both an understanding and acceptance of the spirit of value pluralism. As he himself puts it, "Political activity is important not because there are no absolute ideals or things worth doing for themselves, but because, in ordinary human judgment, there are many of these things. Political morality does not contradict any belief in ideal conduct; it merely sets the stage on which people can, if they wish, argue such truths without degrading these truths into instruments of governmental coercion" (1993, 154).

Moreover, Crick's conception of politics is helpful to us in understanding the practical role that politics can play in dealing with value or moral conflict. First, his conception of politics makes it clear that, regardless of whether or not we might accept value pluralism as conceptually true, the practice of politics has historically involved a recognition, either by a ruler or ruling group, that the society they rule is sufficiently complex so that the ends or values held by one group of citizens in society can be expected to come into conflict with the values held by others, a recognition that there is a variety, as Crick terms it, of conflicting "moral ends," "moral viewpoints," "different truths" which must be reconciled. The practice of politics involves a recognition, as a practical rather than a conceptual matter, that there is, within that complex society, no "absolute ideal," no "authoritative allocation of values," no "allegedly objective 'general will' or 'public interest' " that alone might command sufficient consensus to ensure support for—or at least neutralize effective resistance to—the ruler's actions. As such, the practice of politics rests on a practical understanding that there exists no monist ideology, no monist doctrine or tradition, which is available to that society that is capable, at least on its own, of holding the society together. Indeed, if such a monist ideology, doctrine, or tradition were available to the society, then any conflict as to what the ruler or rulers should do would evaporate, so that, as Crick puts it, "politics would . . . be unnecessary" (1993, 64). It is in this practical sense, therefore, that the practice of politics within a society presumes the existence of some measure of value pluralism. To put this another way, while philosophers may debate the conceptual truth of value pluralism, those who are involved in the practice of politics in modern complex societies come to learn that they must deal with it as a working reality. As Stuart Hampshire explains, "In many societies, and particularly in modern states, the difference between ways of life within a single society cannot plausibly be represented as contributing to a common good. The different ways of life are buttressed by contrary and irreconcilable beliefs, usually religious, but sometimes also purely moral. In any large and economically developed society there will be a battle, not only of interests, but also of contrary moral ideals, passionately defended" (1989, 72–73).

Second, in encouraging a style of governance on the basis of conciliation rather than force, politics, as conceived by Crick, helps to protect value pluralism by encouraging the consideration of a broader range of values or conceptions of the good in government decision making than would be the case in its absence, and by making more difficult the imposition of one group's particular set of values on others. Of course, this is not to argue that the real-world practice of politics has historically guaranteed or, for that matter, can ever guarantee the protection of any particular set of interests or values or prevent the oppression of some groups by others. We can appreciate but should never romanticize politics. Rather, my point is simply to suggest that value pluralism is more likely to survive in a community under a system of politics, as opposed to a system of tyranny or totalitarianism that relies upon force rather than conciliation to resolve the conflicts in values that arise within it. In other words, a political form of governance clearly makes it more difficult—although certainly never impossible—for a ruler or ruling group to practice a monist approach to governance. This is because it permits different groups the opportunity to articulate their different and sometimes conflicting values and because it discourages the use of coercion by government in settling differences among those groups.

Third, because politics makes possible a demarcation between what is considered a public matter and what is considered a private matter (albeit a demarcation that is certainly always negotiable, always shifting and contingent), politics allows different individuals and groups, in pursuing their own particular interests and conceptions of the good, a certain degree of what Berlin once termed "negative freedom," that is to say, the freedom that simply "consists in not being prevented in choosing as I do by other men" (1969, 131). Politics provides a zone of privacy within which individuals and groups can make their own choices regarding incompatible and incommensurable moral ends and can pursue their own particular conceptions of the good without excessive interference from others. In doing this, politics therefore not only provides a greater opportunity for, as noted above, the public pursuit of a broad range of moral ends. It also provides greater opportunities for the private pursuit of such ends. In other words, politics can allow for the exercise of what William Galston calls "expressive liberty," the liberty both of "individuals and groups leading their lives as they see fit, within a broad range of legitimate variation, in accordance with their own understanding of what gives life meaning and value" (2002, 3). In allowing for the exercise of freedom, both public and private, politics can serve, then, to protect and foster value pluralism.

Finally, politics serves to protect value pluralism simply because it helps to maintain the peace among conflicting groups in society without which the pursuit of a wide range of values or conceptions of the good would be difficult, if not impossible. This is because, as Hampshire reminds us, politics, properly conceived, serves as "a protection against the perennial evils of human life" including "the destructions and mutilations of war, poverty, and starvation, enslavement and humiliation" (2000, xi), all of which are serious impediments to the pursuit of most conceptions of the good with the exception, perhaps, of a glorious death. As Hobbes expressed it best, without peace "there is no place for industry; because the fruit thereof is uncertain: and consequently no culture of the earth; no navigation, nor use of the commodities that may be imported by sea; no commodious living; no instruments of moving, and removing, such things as require much force; no knowledge of the face of the earth; no account of time; no arts; no letters; no society; and which is worst of all, continual fear, and danger of violent death; and the life of man, solitary, poor, nasty, brutish, and short" (1962, 100). In other words, without the peace that politics helps to secure and maintain, there can be little room for the pursuit of many of the different and conflicting values or moral ends that we have come to believe as important to us, little room for the idea and practice of value pluralism.

All of this is not to suggest that there is necessarily any logical link between value pluralism and the sort of political pluralism that is implicit in our traditional ideas and practices of politics. One cannot, on the basis of value pluralism alone, logically rule out the use of force and violence as an acceptable and necessary means of resolving conflicts among moral ends. Indeed, any attempt to do so would itself be to advocate a form of monism, one in which the resolution of value conflict by peaceful means was seen as an overriding good that should take priority over all other conceptions of the good on all occasions. The claim made here is simply that an aversion to the use of force and violence in resolving conflicts is a common conception of the good that we happen to share across many different cultures with very different systems of values, both for its own sake and because it often makes easier the pursuit of a variety of other moral ends, and that, at least within our admittedly local, particularistic, and contingent historical experience, politics has been seen as generally helpful in promoting this particular conception of the good.

Conclusion

Politics and value pluralism are therefore strongly connected, if not inextricably linked, to one another. It is, of course, possible that value pluralism could be better protected by some enlightened despot, but, as history continues to remind us, enlightened despots are hard to come by. In light of this, it can be argued that, notwithstanding its sometimes shabby compromises, its uncertainties, and its sharp conflicts, politics can, in fact, help to promote moral conduct. By encouraging government officials to respond to the views of different groups in society, politics makes it more likely that the actions of officials will reflect the different values or conceptions of the good that are held by those groups. By allowing individuals and groups some degree of freedom to make their own choices in their private actions, and also by helping to maintain peace among them, politics makes it more likely that the actions of individuals and groups will reflect the different values that those individuals and groups hold to be important to them. Moreover, politics is a constant reminder to both governments and the citizens they rule that we all have to make choices between conflicting ends, not simply choices about the best means to accomplish a given end. In other words, it is a reminder of our moral responsibility for our actions. It is in these ways, then, that politics helps to promote moral conduct.

4
Politics and the Limitations of a Science of Governance

Notwithstanding the virtues of politics that were claimed in the previous chapter, the sentiment has persisted that there must surely exist some better, some more scientific way of dealing with the various conflicts of interests and values that arise among us as human beings, one that would either substitute for or perhaps at the very least usefully augment the practice of politics. Indeed, as was indicated in chapter 1, our own field of public administration is strongly rooted in an aspiration to make available to society not merely a science of administration but also, more broadly, a science of governance. The latest to share in this aspiration are writers in the area of public management, who see improving governance through the application of social science as a way to earn government "the respect of citizens who pay for, and whose lives are affected by, its programs and regulatory activities" (Lynn, Heinrich, and Hill 2000, 234). This is unquestionably a noble aspiration. However, as I shall argue in this chapter, a scientific approach to the study of governance, such as is advocated by these public management writers, at least when taken alone gives insufficient weight to its inherently political character. This is because it presumes an instrumental rationalist and determinist vision of the process of governance that downplays the conflicts among different values and conceptions of the good, as well as the uncertainty, that are an inherent part of the way in which we have come to govern ourselves. As a result, as I argue here, a scientific approach to governance may not be as helpful to the practice of public administration or governance as its advocates suggest. Moreover, if such an approach were ever to be taken too seriously by public administrators and other government officials, to the point of excluding other more humanistic approaches, it could even become damaging to the practice of governance.

A Science of Governance

In order to understand the problems that are associated with the idea of a so-cial science of governance, it is useful to begin by examining, as an example, the language that public management scholars Laurence Lynn, Carolyn Hein-rich, and Carolyn Hill choose to employ in their article on governance and public management (2000). Lynn, Heinrich, and Hill argue, in this article, for the development of what they term a "logic of governance," one that they see as helpful in addressing, among other things, (1) how "goals such as efficiency or high reliability" can "be incorporated into an existing governance regime so as to promote its success," (2) how a governance regime can "be designed to in-sure priority in resource allocation and attention to particular goals and objec-tives," (3) how "dispersed governance regimes (across states, across municipali-ties within a state, across local offices or networks)" can "be induced to converge on the achievement of particular policy objectives," and (4) how governance can "be organized to ensure greater competence or attention to particular pri-orities" (235–36). These authors claim their model of governance, which they go to great pains to express in terms of a reduced-form mathematical equation, can help determine how "more administrative entities" can "be made to perform like the best of them perform" and how to "ensure accountability and good practice across diverse service units in dispersed locations" (234). They express the hope that their approach will encourage investigators to use what they call "appropri-ate theoretical and statistical models to specify and subsequently identify signifi-cant causal relationships that link governance and performance" (247).

In reflecting upon this inspirational language, the following is worth not-ing. First, in sharp contrast to the concept of politics developed in the previous chapter, the language used by Lynn, Heinrich, and Hill suggests that they do not see governance as involved primarily in the reconciliation of different ends or values. Rather, they seem to view governance in largely instrumental rational-ist terms. Governance, for them, is simply a means of pursuing some previously agreed upon set of particular goals, objectives, or priorities, the achievement of which can then be evaluated scientifically in terms of some scale or measure of performance. Governance is not about how to reconcile conflicting ends or ob-jectives. It is about how "to converge on the achievement of particular policy objectives." To use Michael Oakeshott's term, government here is seen as essen-tially "teleocratic" or purpose-driven, "the management of a purposive concern" (1975, 205–6). Second, the language employed by these authors indicates that they view governance as a largely deterministic system, one in which, with the proper application of social science techniques, we can, to use their words, "en-sure" certain desirable outcomes, such as "attention to particular priorities" and in which there are "significant causal relationships" that connect governance to performance. A social science approach to governance is desirable here so that administrative entities can, in their words, not simply be encouraged but "be made to perform like the best of them." The message that is strongly intimated here is that the men and women who are actually involved in the process of governance can all be regarded, at least for purposes of scientific understanding, as objects subject to general causal laws and that their actions, as dependent variables, are not free but rather are to be explained and predicted in terms of factors outside their control. The exception to this deterministic view of human action are those elected and appointed officials who presumably are free to set the goals, objectives, and priorities of governance as they see fit, those that Lynn, Heinrich, and Hill term the "enacting coalition" (2000, 237–39).

In summary, whatever may be their own beliefs on these matters, the language that Lynn, Heinrich, and Hill choose to employ expresses both an instrumental rationalist and a deterministic vision of the process of governance. In adopting this language, it can be argued here that Lynn and his colleagues often appear as if they wished somehow to escape both the moral and empirical contingencies that arise in the actions of those who participate in governance. In seeking to eliminate such contingencies, these public management writers come close to embracing what Oakeshott once termed a "demonstrative political discourse," a form of political discourse that aspires to "prove the 'correctness' or the 'incorrectness' of a proposal to respond to a political situation in a certain manner" (1991, 83). The hope conveyed here, at least if their more ambitious rhetoric is to be taken seriously, is that there is information available that would somehow, as Oakeshott puts it, "enable us to predict, instead of conjecturing, the consequences of different decisions before they were acted upon, and which would enable us to prove the 'correctness' of our judgments about what is desirable and undesirable to be done or to be endured on any occasion" (82). What seems to be sought in their instrumental rationalist and deterministic vision of governance is an emancipation of "political deliberation from mere opinion and conjecture" (92). However, to be fair to Lynn, Heinrich, and Hill, while these authors may express this instrumental rationalist and deterministic vision of governance with perhaps unusual clarity and enthusiasm, such a vision itself should not be thought of as being, by any means, unique within our field. To the contrary, such instrumental rationalism and determinism would seem implicit in the application of mainstream social science to governance.

Instrumental Rationalism and Social Science

With respect to instrumental rationalism, since mainstream social science cannot determine the ultimate validity of any particular ends or values, the appropriate and, in fact, the only way to evaluate the "goodness" or "correctness" of an action from a scientific point of view is to determine the extent to which it promotes the attainment of a given end or some mutually consistent set of ends. Herbert Simon recognized this quite clearly some half century ago when, in advancing a social science of administration, he argued for what he called "a practical science of administration" that would consist of "propositions as to how men would behave if they wished their activity to result in the greatest attainment of administrative objectives with scarce means" (1957, 253). As Simon saw it, "the central concern for administrative theory" was to be "the rationality of decisions—that is, their appropriateness for the accomplishment of specified goals" (240). In other words, Simon sought a value-free science of administration that would still be useful to practice in that, while exclusively concerned with facts, it would nevertheless permit the evaluation of administrative actions and institutions in instrumental terms. From such an instrumental rationalist perspective, to use Simon's words, an administrative decision is "correct if it selects appropriate means to reach designated ends" (61). According to Simon, "given a complete set of value and factual premises, there is only one decision . . . that is preferable to the others" (223). Consistent with this view, efficiency was for Simon "a guiding criterion in administrative decision" (65). The function of the public administrator was simply "to maximize the attainment of the governmental objectives . . . by the efficient employment of the limited resources . . . available to him" (186–87).

Though by no means embraced universally by public administration scholars, Simon's instrumental rationalist vision of governance and administration has had a significant and continuing influence on our field. In fact, as critics of the mainstream literature such as Jay White and Guy Adams point out, "technical rationality is the one narrative that seems to persist for public administration" (1995, 6). For example, Simon's approach to administrative theory has inspired some scholars to advocate the development of what they term an interdisciplinary "design science" of public administration, a science that would seek improved designs through interdisciplinary research not only at the task level and the organizational level, but also at a constitutional level. For such scholars, "the role of the field is to design and evaluate institutions, mechanisms, and processes that convert collective will and public resources into social profit," and "the best 'design' would be that institution with the cumulative potential to attain preset goals" (Shangraw and Crow, 1989, 156).

Simon's instrumental rationalist vision of social science is also evident within the field of public policy analysis. Edith Stokey and Richard Zeckhauser, in an early classic textbook on the subject, express such a vision forcibly when they indicate that their approach to public policy analysis is "that of the rational decision maker who lays out goals and uses logical processes to explore the best way to reach those goals" and it does not consider "situations in which several decision makers with conflicting objectives participate in a decision" (1978, 3). They express a confidence in the value of science in helping to make public policy decisions by drawing upon "analytic techniques in economics, mathematics, operations research and systems analysis" (3).

Of course, it is true that policy analysis has become considerably more sophisticated and more open to different kinds of approaches since Stokey and Zeckhauser wrote their path-breaking text (see, for example, deLeon 1992). Nevertheless, it is notable that Stuart Nagel and C. E. Teasley, in their recent contribution to what is termed a *Handbook of Public Administration*, continue to assert that public policy analysis seeks to "inform the policy maker about the likely future consequences of choosing various alternatives" and, "as such, it often entails defining a set of goals, determining alternative strategies available to achieve them, and determining the relations between those goals and strategies in order to choose the alternative or combination of alternatives that will best achieve those goals" (1998, 507).

Nagel and Teasley argue here that "among the newest and probably the most useful technique available to the public policy analyst" is something they term "multicriteria decision making," a technique that supposedly generates a decision matrix that allows the analyst to quantitatively rank different policy alternatives against weighted multiple policy objectives (510). According to these authors, this new technique "emphasizes the development of policy goals and the selection of relevant decision criteria" and then "guides decision making by suggesting a best choice from among the available policy alternatives" (510).

Moreover, this instrumental rationalist vision of governance is also evident within the field of public management where, as Laurence O'Toole and Kenneth Meier have pointed out recently, "the bulk of this literature frames the emergence of networks in terms of a tendency or necessity to use multiple linked social actors, often multiple organizational actors, to achieve collective purposes" and attention has been directed to such issues as "how to measure and improve network performance . . . through empirical theory" (2004, 681). Consistent with this vision, public management writers have repeatedly emphasized that policy-makers need to develop clear, consistent, and unambiguous goals so as to effectively guide and constrain the actions of public managers. As Sanjay Pandey and James Garnett put it, public management writers worry that "in the absence of a clear hierarchy of preferences, multiple goals [will] lead to goal conflict" (2006, 38). Consequently, "fostering goal clarity has emerged as a key prescription for enhancing the effectiveness of public organizations" (38). Sergio Fernandez and Hal Rainey, in a recent review of the literature on organizational change, for example, emphasize "the importance of clear, specific policy goals" so as to "help ensure that the measures implemented in the field correspond with the formal policy" (2006, 170). From their perspective, "policy ambiguity" should be avoided because it "can sow confusion, allowing public managers to reinterpret the policy and implement it in a fashion that brings about few of the changes that policy makers intended" (170).

This emphasis on the need for goal clarity can also be discerned in the more popular literature on public management where, for example, David Osborne and Ted Gaebler have urged us to move from "rule-driven government . . . locked up by rules and line items" to what they term "mission-driven government" with "mission-driven organizations . . . that turn their employees free to pursue the organization's mission with the most effective methods they can find" (1993, 112–13). This requires, among other things, "hashing out the fundamental purpose of an organization" and "agreeing on one basic mission" (130–31). Osborne and Gaebler are explicitly critical here of what they see as the tendency of our government "to load several different—and often conflicting—missions on each agency" (131). "Public organizations work best," these authors say, "when they have one clear mission" (131).

The Determinism of the Social Sciences

Turning to the issue of determinism in social science, it must be admitted that most social scientists, even those public management writers who advocate a science of governance, do not necessarily regard themselves as determinists. Nonetheless, determinism is arguably implicit in the very idea of a predictive science of human behavior. Peter Berger has observed that, "in terms of social-scientific method, one is faced with a way of thinking that assumes a priori that the human world is a causally closed system," a system in which "freedom as a special kind of cause is excluded" (1963, 123). Gabriel Almond and Stephen Genco seem to recognize this deterministic perspective when they note that social scientists often express a view of "human behavior as simply reactive and consequently susceptible to the same explanatory logic as 'clocklike' natural phenomena" (1977, 493). James Deese has observed similarly that at "the heart of the behavioral and social sciences" is the "notion that all human action is determined and controlled by causes which operate upon individual human beings" (1985, 1–2). Deese notes here that, in political science, for example, "whether it is in the study of some grand political system or some parochial part of it, the assumption is that the actions of those who engage in politics are caused and therefore open to prediction and control" (7). In other words, the message conveyed by much of the social sciences is, in principle at least, that we all can be regarded as essentially objects subject to general causal laws and that our experiences and actions can be viewed as dependent variables that can be explained and predicted in terms of factors outside our control.

This deterministic vision of human action is expressed with perhaps unusual candor in a popular introductory textbook in social science research methods written originally in the 1970s by Earl Babbie. Babbie argues,

> The deterministic posture of the social sciences represents its most significant departure from more traditional, humanistic examinations of social behavior. Whereas a biographer, for example, might consider the soul-searching and agonies by which a given man will weigh the relative merits and demerits of a given action, arriving at a considered decision, the social scientists would more typically look for the general determinants of such a decision among different aggregates of persons. Where the biographer would argue that the decision reached by each individual person represented the outcome of an idiosyncratic process, the social scientist would say it could be fit into a much simpler, general pattern. (1975, 36)

According to Babbie, in contrast to "the free-will image of man and his behavior" that "suggests that each person is the master of his own destiny, the captain of his own fate," and "makes an individual choice reflecting his own volition," the deterministic perspective of social science suggests "that such choices are the result of factors over which the individual has no control" (365). Noting in a later work how, in response to suggestions from colleagues, he actually dropped this discussion of the issue of determinism from his textbook, Babbie wrote that the issue of determinism is one of "the most sensitive issues of social research—so sensitive, in fact, that it is almost never discussed" (1986, 43). As Babbie candidly admits, "Determinism is an embarrassment for social scientists. It is a fundamental paradigm for nearly all of our research, yet none of us wants to speak out on its behalf. Closer to the bone, our livelihoods depend on determinism, and yet we hope it isn't true. Crudely put, social research assumes a deterministic paradigm that fundamentally denies the existence of free will" (43).

Simon himself expresses such a deterministic perspective when he asserts that "a general theory of administration must include principles of organization that will insure correct decision-making" and "effective action" (1957, 1). In examining the psychological components of such a theory, he observes that "in actual behavior, . . . decision is initiated by stimuli which channel attention in definite directions" and that "a great many stimuli for decision come from outside the individual" (91). Such stimuli, to use Simon's words, "determine what decisions the administrator is likely to make" (92). Moreover, Simon expresses optimism that these stimuli "can themselves be controlled so as to serve broader ends, and a sequence of individual decisions can be integrated into a well-conceived plan" (109). He believed that "the behavior of a rational person can be controlled . . . if the value and factual premises upon which he bases his decision are specified for him" (223).

More recently, Kevin Wagner and Jeff Gill have intimated a deterministic approach to the study of public administration when, in advancing their ideas for a Bayesian approach to public administration research, they argue that what is needed in our field is the "pursuit of underlying causal phenomena" by means of "formal or statistical methods" (2005, 7). Fernandez and Rainey argue, similarly, how "sound causal theory" is "crucial for organizational change" (2006, 170) and that, in order to help practitioners, researchers should employ "multivariate statistical techniques and large-sample data sets of organizations at different levels of government and in different public management settings" (2006, 173). Also, Gregory Daneke, in arguing for a revival of systems theories, seemingly expresses great optimism about the potential results of a deterministic approach when he asks us to "imagine if the same nonlinear devices used to detect credit card fraud were looking for behavioral aberrations amid particular groups prior to September 11, 2001" (2005, 102). According to Daneke, "Other less perilous unraveling of Gordian knots of complex social causation may still yield appreciable improvements in the human condition" (102).

Politics and Social Science

An instrumental rationalist and deterministic approach to human action, therefore, is far from uncommon in our field. However, when applied to governance, this approach is deeply problematic because it appears to allow little, if any, room for the practice of politics in governance. If we accept, as public management scholars Lynn, Heinrich, and Hill rightly remind us, that "governance is inherently political" (2000, 236), then it is a process in which those who govern must often seek to reconcile conflicting ends and values rather than simply finding the most efficient and effective means of pursuing some agreed upon set of ends or goals. Moreover, an inherently political form of governance is one in which the meanings of such terms as *efficiency, performance,* and even *effectiveness* are inherently ambiguous and, as such, not readily susceptible to any sort of precise scientific evaluation. In fact, these terms can only have any sort of precise meaning for governance in a world in which the ends sought by those who govern are compatible and commensurable with one another. Should these ends, in fact, turn out to be incompatible and incommensurable with one another, then an instrumental rationalist approach simply cannot provide administrators with any guidance in choosing among them.

Simon, to his credit, recognizes this problem when he argues that unless the activities of an organization are "directed toward exactly the same value, measurement of results cannot tell which course of action is preferable" (1957, 176). His suggested remedy for this problem is to fix "the relative weights of conflicting values" (176). Where an agency pursues two conflicting aims, "in balancing the one aim against the other, and in attempting to find a common denominator" it is "necessary to cease thinking of the two aims as ends in themselves, and instead to conceive them as means to some more general end" (7). More broadly, Simon would have us think of different combinations of competing values in terms of the economist's idea of "utility surfaces" or indifference curves that map the trade-offs between different values (73).

At first glance, at least to those social scientists already sympathetic to Simon's instrumental rationalism, this approach to dealing with conflicting ends or values might seem quite sensible. However, such an approach is actually fraught with problems. For one thing, Simon's references here to "relative weights of conflicting values," to finding a "common denominator" for conflicting aims, and to "utility surfaces" would seem to posit the availability of precisely the type of overarching common standard of value or measuring rod for conflicting values that value pluralism denies us. Thus, his approach ignores the difficult moral conflicts between rival and incommensurable values or conceptions of the good that, as pointed out in chapter 2, are often experienced by public policy-makers and administrators. Moreover, Simon's argument makes even clearer for us the point that politics, as we have defined it here, has little, if any, role to play in an instrumental rationalist approach to governance. This is because if there were ever really a consensus about what should be "the relative weights of conflicting values" or about the "common denominators" for conflicting aims or, for that matter, if there were really some sort of "utility surfaces" shared by all citizens, then we would already have, in fact, achieved what David Easton terms an "authoritative allocation of values for a society" (Easton 1953, 129), and given this remarkable achievement, there would no longer be any need for politics in government, only well-trained managers to implement the means necessary to the attainment of those values.

Finally, if we accept that governance is inherently political, then it is a process in which the actions of those involved are essentially free and, as a result, outcomes must be inherently uncertain. Contrary to the deterministic conception of human behavior that is, at the very least, implicit in the social scientific approach, the connection between the practice of politics and the existence of freedom, discussed earlier, makes clear the ineluctable element of uncertainty or contingency that must enter into any predictions that social scientists might wish to offer regarding human actions in political matters. As Crick himself argues, the thing about liberty is that it is "an exuberant and unpredictable thing" so that "the actions of free men are always unpredictable" ([1962] 1993, 214). Indeed, "when everything is knowable, determined, or certain, freedom is impossible" (55). Rejecting any aspirations to a deterministic science of politics, Crick observes that "the basic philosophical concept of a free action" is "an unpredictable action (one not logically entailed or determined by any necessary circumstances)" (261). This has important implications, for it means that in political negotiations within the process of governance, for example, "no one will get all they want or even quite what they expect" because "precise outcomes in difficult situations are unpredictable" (261). In fact, as Crick notes, "only in efficient autocracies are the outcomes of 'negotiations' predictable" (261). More broadly, it means that since the practice of politics facilitates freedom of action, "political knowledge is always tentative" and that one "cannot hope to find scientific laws without excluding politics" (182). In other words, if politics is to be practiced in a meaningful fashion, men and women must be free to choose and, therefore, their actions, to a significant degree, must be uncertain and not subject to prediction by social science.

Implications for Administrative Practice

In summary, therefore, because of its instrumental rationalist and deterministic view of human action, the social scientific approach to governance that is advocated by public management writers, as well as by others within our field, would seem to downplay, if not actually deny, its essentially political character. This is important because, if true, it raises serious questions about the practicality of such an approach within our highly political form of governance. In particular, practitioners who seek guidance in our political system of governance as to how to reconcile conflicting ends or values or how to deal with free and unpredictable human beings would not seem likely to find much use in a scientific approach that emphasizes instrumental rationality and determinism.

In this regard it is noteworthy that, despite the passage of several centuries since the idea of a modern science of governance first emerged, its contributions to the practice of governance have, so far at least, been relatively modest. As Charles Lindblom has put it, there is an "absence of undeniable evidence" in the social sciences and it is difficult to "identify a single social science finding or idea that is undeniably indispensable to any social task or effort" (1990, 136). Also, Richard Rorty has argued that the assumption that a "thin 'behavioristic' vocabulary" for the social sciences would somehow facilitate the "prediction and control" of social situations "has not panned out very well" (1982, 197). In his view, "the last fifty years of research in the social sciences have not notably increased our predictive abilities" (197). Even Carolyn Heinrich, who, as noted earlier, has advocated much greater use of social science in public management and policy, concedes in a recent article that "one of the most disconcerting . . . discoveries of our far-reaching efforts to promote evidence-based policy making and improve government performance" is that "the more we have come to know, the more aware we are of how tentative, limited, and somewhat erroneous the bases of our information and evidence are" (2007, 274). In other words, the re-cord of the social sciences in contributing to public administration and policy is just not that impressive and certainly not so strong as to indicate that we should substantially shift our scholarly efforts, let alone invest all of these efforts, in the direction of a more scientific approach to governance and administration.

Moreover, it is far from clear that most public administration practitioners themselves have been able to find very much guidance from the instrumental rationalist and deterministic vocabulary of mainstream social science. To the contrary, as Richard Box has argued, practitioners often "feel that the writing of academicians is removed from the needs of daily practice" (1992, 65). As he notes, there is little evidence that practitioners "crave research containing find-ings embedded in multiple regression equations, factor analyses, or similar tech-niques" (65). Laurence Lynn, exhibiting perhaps a less sympathetic view, writes how, among practitioners, "a collective glazing over of eyes in classrooms greets professorial efforts to apply 'theory'" and how "far more welcome are trenchant, engaging stories" (1996, 141). Lynn attributes this attitude to anxiety and conser-vatism on the part of practitioners. He argues, perhaps somewhat patronizingly, that "a display of contempt for theory may . . . mask insecurity or, worse, an un-pleasant truth; some practitioners believe that others need to change but they do not" (142). However, even conceding that both academics and practitioners are all prone, on occasion, to some intellectual laziness, might it not also be the case that the instrumental rationalism and determinism that are characteristic of sci-entific approaches to governance and administration simply do not fit very well with the ordinary lived experiences of practitioners? As Isaiah Berlin has argued more generally, a resistance among practitioners to an "unswerving devotion to mathematical methods" in political affairs "may partly be due to natural conser-vatism, hatred of change, unconscious adherence to 'common-sense' theories of their own, . . . unthinking faith in and loyalty to the old establishment, however cruel, unjust, grotesque. But the whole of the resistance to this doctrine is not attributable to stupidity and mediocrity and vested interests and prejudices and narrow egoism and ignorance and superstition; in part it is due to beliefs about what kind of behaviour does and what kind of behaviour does not tend to pro-duce successful results" (1996, 32).

Furthermore, if many public administration practitioners evince a lack of enthusiasm for a scientific approach to governance, this may not altogether be a bad thing. Were practitioners, in fact, ever to take too seriously the idea of a scientific approach to governance—at least to the point of excluding other more humanistic approaches—then this idea might actually end up being harmful to the practice of governance and administration. This is because the rhetoric of both instrumental rationalism and determinism that is employed by social scientists tends to devalue moral responsibility. The rhetoric of instrumental rationalism in public administration devalues moral responsibility because it deflects the attention of administrators away from the fact that they must often face difficult choices among competing and incommensurable moral ends. It hides moral choices from the view of administrators by focusing their attention single-mindedly on technical questions about how best to accomplish some predefined set of measurable goals, missions, or ends. In doing so, instrumental rationalism, when practiced in government, can promote the dangerous kind of monism, previously discussed in chapter 2, in which the ends pursued by administrators can be seen as justifying almost any means, however inhumane or barbaric. Such instrumental rationalism can lead and has led, as Stuart Hampshire argues, to "persecutions, massacres, and wars, . . . coolly justified by calculations of the long range benefit to mankind," and it even encourages "political pragmatists, in the advanced countries, using cost-benefit analyses prepared for them by gifted professors, [to] continue to burn and destroy" (1983, 84–85).

Of course, this does not mean that public administration scholars themselves are totalitarians of the type that Berlin had in mind when he wrote of those responsible for the sacrifice "of living human beings on the altars of abstractions" (1992, 16). Nor is it even to argue that these scholars are self-consciously monistic in their own moral thinking. Rather, the argument advanced here is simply that the instrumental rationalism characteristic of those public administration writers who advance a science of governance can, sometimes, encourage monist ways of thinking and acting and, in doing so, can erode our sense of moral responsibility. In this respect, even if we see ourselves as firmly committed to the ideals of liberal democracy and political pluralism, perhaps we need, at the same time, as Michel Foucault once warned us, to be wary of "the fascism in us all, in our heads, and in our everyday behavior" (2000b, 108).

The rhetoric of determinism in public administration further devalues moral responsibility because it can foster the idea that those whom the administrator must deal with—citizens, politicians, and other administrators—are not human beings as such but are merely objects to be manipulated at will. Hanna Pitkin recognizes this danger when she argues, "the costs of coming to see men too often or too exclusively as human objects are multiple" (1993, 321). According to Pitkin,

First and most obviously, the experience is likely to bear fruit in action; conceiving men as objects, we are increasingly likely to treat them that way. This need not mean doing them harm. . . . But it does allow us to do harm with a minimum of guilt. It does not mean treating men immorally so much as treating them amorally, in a manner in which morality plays no role. As individuals, we become increasingly incapable of the moral attitude. . . . On the social and political level, we think in terms of "social engineering," manipulatively; we see the problem as one of channeling men, by neutral, administrative measures. Feeling that we know the real, objective causes of others' actions and social condition, we no longer need to listen to their views; feeling that we can determine their needs scientifically, we become impatient with their wants. Both individually and socially, human relations are resolved into technical problems. (321)

Moreover, determinism can erode administrators' sense of moral responsibility for their own choices by tempting them to attribute their actions to forces that they cannot control. It can promote what Berger, drawing on Jean-Paul Sartre, has termed "bad faith," that is, "to pretend something is necessary that is in fact voluntary" (1963, 143). Indeed, we should note here that, as Berlin warns, determinism has a certain appeal to those who wield government power in that it devolves "the responsibility for a great many things that people do on to impersonal causes, and therefore leaves them in a sense unblameworthy for what they do" (2000, 19). Once a person accepts determinism, an endless array of excuses becomes available for most any action:

When I make a mistake, or commit a wrong or a crime, or do anything else which I recognize, or which others recognize, as bad or unfortunate, I can say, "How could I avoid it?—that was the way I was brought up" or "That is my nature, something for which natural laws are responsible" or "I belong to a society, a class, a Church, a nation, in which everyone does it, and nobody seems to condemn it" or "I am psychologically conditioned by the way in which my parents behaved to each other and to me, and by the economic and social circumstances in which I was placed, or was forced into, not to be able to choose to act otherwise" or, finally, "I was under orders." (19–20)

The foregoing discussion is not to deny, of course, the possibility that at some point in the future we may find that determinism may, after all, turn out to be true. Rather, it is simply to ask, from a merely pragmatic point of view and in light of our current knowledge, whether or not, given the coercive power that government can exercise over our lives, we really want our government leaders, including public administrators, to adopt with zealous enthusiasm a social scientific vocabulary that, implicitly at least, denies the possibility of freedom and moral responsibility. As Rorty argues, the question here is not whether the "Behaviorese" that is characteristic of mainstream social science "could not catch what [people are] 'really' doing" (1982, 198). Rather, it is that such "Behaviorese" is simply "not a good vocabulary for moral reflection. We just don't want to be the sort of policy-makers who use those terms for deciding what to do to our fellow-humans" (198).

In short, there is a danger that both the instrumental rationalism and the determinism that are so prominent in social science discourse could contribute to an erosion of a sense of moral responsibility among public administrators for their actions. However, even if we discount this danger, perhaps the greatest risk here is that an enthusiasm for a scientific approach to governance, if not adequately checked by other perspectives, might breed a certain disdain or contempt for the practice of politics and the constraints that such politics impose upon the exercise of power. In this respect, it is worth noting that those scholars in public administration who have embraced the idea of a science of administration have also often been critical of the highly political character of American governance and, moreover, have been hostile to the types of constitutional institutions that give it this political character, seeing them as little more than an impediment to efficient and effective government (Spicer 1995). For instance, Meier, whose work was noted earlier, has complained how "at times policies have contradictory goals" that "are left to the bureaucracy to grapple with as best it can" (196). As he puts it, "we now demand . . . that bureaucracy . . . respond to political demands whether or not those demands are consistent" (196). Not content with merely administrative reforms, Meier believes that we need to "redesign our political system to resolve rather than exacerbate conflict" (197). He criticizes the founders' constitutional "procedural checks" because "they prevent the resolution of political conflicts and the adoption of [what he sees as] good public policy," and he suggests furthermore that we might examine "the more unified political structures and corporatist processes of many European countries" so as to find ways to "instill in politicians a responsibility for the performance of political institutions as a whole" (197). Not lacking in ambition, Meier also recommends that we hold less frequent elections in order "to change the time frame considerations of electoral institutions" and that "we restrict and perhaps even eliminate political appointees" (197).

Interestingly enough, Meier advances this rather ambitious agenda for radical constitutional reform here without the benefit of any support at all from the "rigorous quantitative approaches" that he, along with his colleague Jeff Gill, have urged upon us as part of their "methodological manifesto" for public administration (Gill and Meier 2000, 195). However, leaving this methodological oversight aside, what Meier's argument perhaps illustrates best is how, at least among academics, enthusiasm for a scientific approach to governance is often associated with a disdain toward the role of ordinary politics in governance and also toward those constitutional institutions that help protect and enhance that role. His sharply anti-political rhetoric here brings to mind Crick's observation that "at heart, what disturbs those hopeful for a science of politics is simply the element of conflict in ordinary politics" (1993, 96). It also leads us to ask whether or not we would really want practitioners in government to share his enthusiasm for a "rigorous" scientific approach to governance if it risks promoting, among them, the same lack of affection for politics and constitutionalism that he so clearly expresses. It is quite one thing to have a group of prominent academic writers expound among themselves in articles and at conferences about the virtues of a scientific approach to governance and the defects of our highly political form of governance. It would be quite another thing were such attitudes embraced uncritically by government officials, elected or appointed, who actually have power over our lives.

Conclusion

A scientific approach to governance, therefore, is problematic for public administration in that, in promoting an instrumental rationalist and deterministic view of governance, it ignores the conflicting ends and values and the freedom that we have come to experience as part and parcel of our own tradition of politics. In doing so, it provides a view of governance that is, at best, not always very helpful to practitioners and, at worst, potentially dangerous to governance in that, if it were the dominant view with little or no counterweight, it might devalue a sense of moral responsibility among practitioners and encourage a lack of appreciation among them for the virtues of politics in dealing with conflicts among competing values and interests and in protecting freedom. Oakeshott probably summarizes the matter best when he warns us that "a craving for demonstrative political argument may corrupt us by suggesting that we have not got to make choices, sometimes on little more than the courage of our convictions, or by suggesting that we can pass off the responsibility for making these choices upon some axiom or 'law' for which, in turn, we have no responsibility" (1991, 95). According to Oakeshott, such a craving can "make us discontented with ordinary political discourse which, because it is not demonstrative, we may be tempted to regard as a species of unreason" (95). Consequently, we should be cautious before adopting or urging practitioners to adopt, to use Crick's words, a technological "style of thought" that promises to "rescue mankind from the lack of certainty and the glut of compromises in politics" (92).

In assessing all of these risks, it is worth remembering that the desire for a predictive science of human behavior, or, frankly, even for simply the outward appearance of such a science, is not entirely unconnected with the desire for power. Alasdair MacIntyre, for example, has reminded us how managers, both in the public and private sector, have sought to "justify themselves and their claims to authority, power and money by invoking their own competence as scientific managers of social change" (1984, 86). Such justification becomes easier when, as MacIntyre notes, social science is seen "as providing a stock of law-like generalizations with strong predictive power" (88). Where there exists in society a widespread belief in a predictive social science, there is a danger therefore that public administrators may use that belief—whether or not it is warranted—to justify the power that they exercise over their subordinates and citizens.

All of this is not to suggest that social scientists should not seek to investigate governance using the techniques of mainstream social science or that students in public administration should not be educated in such techniques. To the contrary, as Berlin notes, "whatever can be isolated, looked at, inspected, should be. We need not be obscurantist" (1996, 48). Whatever its limits, it must be conceded that the practice of conventional empiricist social science gives concrete expression to important values that we should pay attention to in the discourse of governance and public administration, for example, those of a certain degree of impartiality, openness to criticism, and a willingness to learn from empirical experience. This seems to be the view of Mel Dubnick, who, in seeking to defend positivism, argues that what modern social science has to offer public administration is not so much methodological rigor as the cultivation of a "critical 'culture of inquiry'" that is willing to engage in "an ongoing search/ debate over what constitutes credible research" (Bogason et al. 2000, 408). Also, Hugh Miller, one of the leading postmodernist writers in public administration, writes of scientific positivism in general that "its rules of reason and rationality, its openness, and its coherence, are features worthy of admiration rather than condemnation" and "its norms of skeptical inquiry are legendary" (Miller 2003, 17). Furthermore, Rorty, while unimpressed by any claims of science to rationality or objectivity, argues nonetheless that the institutions of science give "concreteness and detail to the idea of 'unforced agreement'" and that "reference to such institutions fleshes out the idea of a free and open encounter" (Rorty 1991, 39). For Rorty, science is valuable as a practical demonstration of the idea that "the best way to find out what to believe is to listen to as many suggestions and arguments as you can" (39). In doing so, "the institutions and practices which make up various scientific communities" provide "suggestions about the way in which the rest of the culture might organize itself" (39). Viewed from this perspective, then, conventional social science can be thought of as what Hugh Miller and Charles Fox have termed "an epistemic community" (2001), one that happens to foster certain traditions and practices that we have come to find helpful to us.

However, the argument presented in this chapter suggests that we should perhaps be more modest in our expectations about the contributions that social science can make to the practice of governance. Moreover, it suggests that we should not all rush headlong with contemporary public management scholars to embrace a scientific approach to the study of governance. We need an alternative approach to governance that properly recognizes that governance is inherently political in the sense that it is concerned with the peaceful resolution of conflict among competing ends or conceptions of the good. We need an approach that also recognizes that because governance is political, administrators will often be faced with making choices among competing ends without recourse to any sort of scientific algorithm and that they have a moral responsibility for these choices. In short, we need a pluralist approach to public administration that recognizes, as Camilla Stivers puts it, that "what makes public life public" are "irreducible differences, out of which we must as a people find a way to live together" (2000b, 17–18). Let us now turn to the development of at least the outlines of such an approach.

5
A Pluralist Approach
to Public Administration

Adversary Argument, Constitutionalism,
and Administrative Discretion

When we think about what might constitute a pluralist approach to public administration, it is useful to begin by examining more closely what exactly it is about politics that makes possible the political conciliation of conflicting interests and values. In this chapter, I shall argue that, at a bare minimum, a political resolution of conflicts among competing values requires some sort of institutionalized and broadly accepted process in which the different sides of a political dispute can make arguments for their particular ends and interests. In other words, we need accepted political practices that provide a measure of "procedural justice" or "fairness." This, in turn, as I argue here, suggests that we Americans must pay special attention to our constitutional traditions both because they have encouraged the resolution of conflict through political practices of adversarial argument and also because they make it impossible for public administrators to avoid their moral responsibility to participate in these practices.

In advancing this argument, I draw significantly on the ideas of Stuart Hampshire. Furthermore, so as to clarify the nature of Hampshire's approach to politics, I shall contrast his approach with the approaches taken by John Rawls and Jürgen Habermas. The writings of both Rawls and Habermas merit special attention here because they have had a significant impact on public administration thinking, albeit mainly among critics of the mainstream. Rawls has provided inspiration for proponents of virtue ethics in public administration such as George Frederickson (1997), whereas Habermas has provided an intellectual underpinning for critical theorists in the field like Robert Denhardt (1981, 2000).

Conflict Resolution and Procedural Justice

For Stuart Hampshire, like Bernard Crick, politics constitutes a set of practices that allow us to avoid the use of force or violence in the resolution of conflicts among differing conceptions of the good that arise between us. As Hampshire notes, it is because "there will always be conflicts between conceptions of the good" that "there is everywhere a well-recognized need for procedures of conflict resolution, which can replace brute force and domination and tyranny" (2000, 5). Such procedures, of course, can take on a wide variety of different institutional forms in different cultures and, also, at different times in history. These have included, for example, such institutions as parliaments, courts, and other assemblies or councils. However, what is common to most—although perhaps not all—of these various institutions is that they typically involve some set of practices for adversarial argument that provides an opportunity for different groups to present and discuss their views on the issues that divide them, a set of practices that meets "the single prescription *audi alteram partem* (hear the other side)" (Hampshire 2000, 8). According to Hampshire,

> In accepting any adversary procedure, the normal case is the man who from the beginning of his adult life finds himself attached to an ethnic group, a social group, a locality, perhaps a religious or moral group, and where each group is in competition with other groups for some degree of dominance in a single society. In such conditions of competition there are two routes by which a person or group may seek to gain its ends: by outright domination, involving force and the threat of force, or, alternatively, by an argumentative procedure within some institution (parliament, law court, assembly) that happens to have come into existence with its own recognized rules of procedure. (17)

Unlike the variety of other values or conceptions of the good that, as discussed in chapter 2, tend to divide us, the idea that we ought to settle disputes among ourselves by means of practices or procedures that allow for adversary argument or "hearing the other side" is a value that seems to command both longstanding and widespread, if not universal, assent. Despite our different cultural backgrounds, our different histories, or, for that matter, our different moral or philosophical outlooks, many of us recognize and appreciate the value of settling disputes by argument rather than by force. As Hampshire observes, "procedures of adjudication, which require the weighing of arguments, are . . . understood and applied across many varieties of barriers: across the frontiers of religious belief, across national loyalties, across philosophical and moral barriers. They are employed, and have been employed throughout history, between hostile powers in negotiation" (1989, 54).

To the degree that these practices of adversarial argument allow some sort of a hearing for the different parties involved in moral conflict, they may be seen as providing an intimation of a minimal norm of "procedural justice" or "fairness." Hampshire recognizes this when he argues that "a rock-bottom and preliminary morality of justice and fair dealing is needed to keep a balance between competing moralities and to support respected procedures of arbitration between them. Otherwise any society becomes an unstable clash of fanaticisms" (1989, 72). This idea of justice, in his view, has always had "a constant connotation and core sense, from the earliest times until the present day," and it "refers to a regular and reasonable procedure of weighing claims and counter-claims, as in an arbitration or court of law" (63).

However, simply because we observe the widespread use of these practices of adversarial argument or procedural justice does not mean that there exists some universal set of just procedures or universal rules for political discourses that are available to resolve the value conflicts that arise among us. To the contrary, the very character of the procedures, which have evolved within a given society at a given time, is inevitably contingent upon its particular historical experience. This is because, in order to earn our respect and for us to feel comfortable with them, these procedures must become familiar to us as part of our accustomed practices of living. As Hampshire points out,

> Human beings are habituated to recognize the rules and conventions of the institutions within which they have been brought up, including the conventions of their family life. Institutions are needed as settings for just procedures of conflict resolution, and [these] institutions are formed by recognized customs and habits, which harden into specific rules of procedure within the various institutions—law courts, parliaments, councils, political parties, and others. The members of any society, and the citizens of any state, at any time and anywhere, normally expect that the conflicts in which they are involved should be settled in accordance with the rules recognized within that particular society or that particular state. (2000, 54)

The exact requirements of procedural justice for any particular society therefore can never be universal but, rather, always "are matters of historical contingency" (Hampshire 2000, 18), and these requirements will "vary immensely in different places and at different times in virtue of local customs and rules" (55).

The only thing that these varied procedures have in common at all with each other, in fact, is that they allow for what is seen as some sort of "a fair hearing to the two or more sides in a conflict" and that the institutions that incorporate these procedures "must have earned, or be earning, respect and recognition from their history in a particular state or society" (55). As a result, in order to determine what is a fair or just way of resolving any particular conflict among conceptions of the good in society, we are always compelled to "refer to the social situation and beliefs and traditions of the particular society at the particular time" (55–56).

Furthermore, in acknowledging the usefulness of our social practices of adversary argument, we should also recognize that the particular institutions and rules that we end up using to adjudicate conflict among ourselves will never be seen as perfect by all parties and will themselves be subject to ongoing argument and modification. As Hampshire emphasizes, "procedures of conflict resolution within any state are always being criticized and are always changing and are never as fair and as unbiased as they ideally might be" (2000, 26). From his perspective, we cannot expect any state to achieve "a perfect fairness in the representation of the conflicting moral outlooks within it" because "procedural justice tends of its nature to be imperfect and not ideal, being the untidy outcome of past political compromises" (31–32). We should not be surprised, therefore, that "the specific forms of argument and negotiation, and the arenas in which the conflicts are to be fought out, are often themselves subjects of dispute" and that they can be "expected to change as the untidy upshot of regular political conflicts" (28–29).

Nor should we suppose here that, just because practices of procedural justice tend to reduce the use of violence, procedural justice is therefore a norm to which we all must adhere in all possible circumstances. To claim this for such practices would be to claim too much. It would, in effect, be to assert procedural justice as some type of a supreme or monist value that trumps all others in all times and places, and thus to deny the very reality of the value conflict that we seek to settle through institutions of procedural justice. We must therefore recognize that procedural justice is not something that must always override all other values or conceptions of the good. We must come to terms with the fact that there will always be exceptional cases in which we must sacrifice even procedural justice in the pursuit of some other good that we deem essential to us. Despite the great importance he attaches to procedural justice as a means of resolving conflict, even Hampshire concedes that there are, on occasion, circumstances in which "considerations of procedural justice . . . ought to be overridden in order that some other essential value . . . may be protected, such as the avoidance of widespread misery or the preservation of life" (2000, 36), or, perhaps, "to defeat an incipient tyranny that would clearly lead to greater injustice" (1989, 140). Procedural justice is not, then, a supreme value but simply an obligation that arises because "men and women need to live together in societies and states of some kind" and because they "encounter persons with contrary moral concerns and with incompatible conceptions of the good, both beyond the actual frontiers of their society and within them" (Hampshire 1989, 140).

If we accept Hampshire's analysis here, our institutions of politics can be seen as constituting the particular historically contingent practices of procedural justice that have happened to evolve in our society for the resolution of conflicts among competing values or conceptions of the good by means of adversary argument rather than force. To claim that our political practices provide a measure of procedural justice is in no way to suggest here that political argument is the same as legal argument or that political institutions provide the same type of procedural justice provided by our courts. To the contrary, as Hampshire argues, "fairness in parliament and in party politics is different from fairness in a law court" (2000, 54–55). This is because political conflicts, as opposed to legal conflicts, often involve "political and ideological enemies arguing against each other, and not professional advocates who at the same time acknowledge a common allegiance to the law of the land" (96). Consequently, in politics, "every appeal to precedent in a political procedural dispute, and every appeal to equality of access, is open to dispute, if it is not already guaranteed by the undisputed law of the land" (97). Nonetheless, despite the significant differences that exist between politics and law, there are also important underlying similarities. As politicians and close observers of politics know only too well, the practice of politics, like that of law, is not without its own set of elaborate procedures that allow for hearing the other side. Crick reminds us of this when he notes that, "since the business of politics is the conciliation of differing interests, justice must not merely be done, but be seen to be done" ([1962] 1993, 148). Inevitably in politics, as Crick puts it, there will be "a complexity of procedures, frustrating to both parties, but ensuring that decisions are not made until all significant objections and grievances have been heard. Procedure . . . enables something to be done, but only after the strength behind the objections has been assessed. . . . Procedures, legal or Parliamentary, . . . tiresome, obstructive, and pettifogging though they may be, at least force great acts of innovation to explain themselves publicly, at least leave doors open for their amendment if the government has misjudged the power of the forces opposed to it" (148).

What political institutions also have in common with judicial institutions is that the effectiveness of both rests upon locally established and respected procedures that provide for the resolution of differences by two-sided adversary argument and that such procedures provide an alterative to the use of force. Without such institutions, as events in a multitude of failed or failing states around the globe make abundantly clear, and as Hampshire himself recognizes, echoing Hobbes, "we should expect catastrophe. Conflicts will then no longer be resolved within the political domain but will be resolved by violence or the threat of violence and life will become nasty, brutish and short. Whatever one's conception of the good, such anarchy will generally be reckoned a great evil, alongside starvation and near-starvation, disease, imprisonment, slavery, and humiliation" (2000, 98).

As such, our institutions of procedural justice, which provide us opportunities for adversarial argument, both judicial and political, are crucial to preserving value pluralism and in limiting the dangers of monism. Without such institutions, "no morality directed towards the greater goods can be applicable and can survive in practice" (Hampshire 1989, 72). Procedural justice, because it helps to avert violence and anarchy, is, to use Hampshire's words, "a necessary support of any morality in which more positive virtues are valued" (72). Moreover, beyond simply preserving the peace, our practices of procedural justice, including those of politics, allow for the public expression of competing conceptions of the good. In doing so, while they cannot always guarantee that decisions reached will take account of these different conceptions, they make this more likely. At the very least, these practices can act as a constraint on the monopolization of political discourse by those groups who would seek to impose their particular moral ends or values on others who do not happen to share them. Richard Rorty clearly appreciates the value of such practices in the protection of a plurality of different moral ends or conceptions of the good when he notes that our current condition of moral and cultural diversity is "just the sort of situation that the Western liberal ideal of procedural justice was *designed* to deal with" (1991, 209). According to Rorty, in recommending procedural justice as an ideal, one need not recommend "a philosophical outlook, a conception of human nature or of the meaning of human life" but, rather, simply "point out the practical advantages of liberal institutions in allowing individuals and cultures to get along together without intruding on each other's privacy, without meddling with each other's conception of the good" (209). As he puts it, "ideals may be local and culture-bound, and nevertheless be the best hope of the species" (208).

Alternative Views of Political Discourse

It may be objected here that Hampshire's notion of procedural justice as simply locally accepted practices of adversary argument provides us with too thin a foundation or basis for thinking normatively about politics and public administration. Some readers, including perhaps some virtue ethicists and critical theorists in public administration, might see Hampshire's notion of political discourse as simply hearing the other side as just too open-ended and insufficiently attentive to justice in that it does not seem to distinguish between what are good and bad arguments. In light of this, it may be helpful to compare Hampshire's approach with some arguably more muscular approaches to political discourse taken by contemporary political philosophers John Rawls and Jürgen Habermas. Both Rawls's and Habermas's approaches clearly exhibit strong similarities to that of Hampshire. All three philosophers share a concern with how we might use practices of argumentation or discourse to settle the conflicts that arise among us in regard to our conceptions of the good in a pluralistic society. However, the approaches taken by Rawls and Habermas differ significantly from that taken by Hampshire in that both of the former seek to identify, in a much more rigorous fashion than does Hampshire, the preconditions they see as necessary for reasoned political argument or discourse.

Rawls, for his part, wants us to "work out a political conception of political justice" for what he admits is "a (liberal) constitutional democratic regime that a plurality of reasonable doctrines, both religious and nonreligious, liberal and nonliberal, may endorse for the right reasons" (1996, xli). Rawls specifically rejects here the idea of a political order as simply a "modus vivendi" arising from "circumstance and exhaustion"; he wants instead a more robust political order, one that employs, as part of an overlapping consensus, "political conceptions such as liberty and equality together with a guarantee of sufficient all-purpose means . . . for citizens to make intelligent and effective use of their freedoms" (xli). Within this political consensus, citizens are assumed to share not only a conception of justice, but also "general beliefs about human nature and the way political and social institutions generally work" and "all such beliefs relevant to political justice" that are supported by "publicly shared methods of inquiry and forms of reasoning" including the "procedures and conclusions of science and social thought, when these are well established and not controversial" (66–67). Furthermore, citizens are to reach such consensus not "by mere rhetoric or persuasion" but "on the basis of mutually recognized criteria and evidence" (111). While citizens in his liberal democratic state certainly may "affirm a diversity of reasonable religious and philosophical doctrines," Rawls argues that such citizens should always be "ready to explain the basis of their actions to one another in terms each could reasonably expect that others might endorse as consistent with their freedom and equality" (218). In short, while we are free to argue with each other in politics, our arguments should, at least, be based on the shared norms of an idealized liberal society.

Habermas, taking a somewhat more radical tack, wants us to achieve a form of democratic discourse that will approximate what he sees as "the ideal conditions of a speech situation specifically immunized against repression and inequality," one in which "the practice of argumentation is characterized by the intention of winning the assent of a universal audience to a problematic proposition in a non-coercive but regulated contest for the better arguments based on the best information and reasons" (1998, 228). Within a proper democratic setting, he sees political argumentation not as a contest among conflicting interests and conceptions of the good but rather as a "cooperative search for truth" (228). This type of political discourse provides the basis for making moral judgments about human actions because, as Habermas puts it, the only reasons for action that could be considered valid from a moral perspective are those "to which all possibly affected persons could assent as participants in rational discourses" (459). Consistent with this quasi-Kantian perspective, Habermas argues, "it must be reasonable to expect those who participate in the legislative process, whether directly or indirectly, to drop the role of private subject" (32). He envisions, as an ideal, a process of lawmaking in which those citizens who participate are, to use his words, "*not* allowed to take part simply in the role of actors oriented to success" in the pursuit of their own private and particularistic agendas (32). Rather, for Habermas, "the democratic procedure of lawmaking relies on citizens' making use of their communicative and participatory rights . . . with an orientation towards the common good" (461). In other words, those participating in political discourse should, first of all, check their personal, group, and organizational loyalties and agendas at the door. Using this approach to political discourse, Habermas develops an argument for what he sees as a democratic but procedural paradigm of law that "no longer favors a particular ideal of society, a particular vision of the good life, or even a particular political option" but "states the necessary conditions under which . . . legal subjects in their role as enfranchised citizens can reach an understanding with one another about what their problems are and how they are to be solved" (445).

While Rawls and Habermas obviously take very different approaches to political discourse, both writers seem focused on the importance of setting preconditions or norms that would govern political argument in such a way as to render it somehow more rational, or at least more reasonable. They believe that political arguments should win not simply because they are more persuasive or attractive to particular audiences but rather because these argument are based, to use their words, on the "right reasons" and on "reasonable doctrines," not "mere rhetoric or persuasion," and because they are supported by established "procedures of science and social thought," or because they are "better arguments based on the best information and reasons." By hemming in what is acceptable political discourse, while both present elegant abstractions of those liberal democratic intuitions and habits of behavior that are characteristic of Western societies, Habermas and Rawls also give the impression of wanting to remove from political argument much of the human conflict and passion that is, in fact, characteristic of real-world politics. In this sense, Rawls and Habermas, in laying out their conditions for effective political discourse, at times resemble, albeit perhaps unintentionally, what Crick terms the "a-political liberal," the liberal who "wishes to enjoy all the fruits of politics" but also likes at the same time to "scrub it down, clean it up, and tether it firmly until this terrier becomes a fairly lifeless, if respectable, lap-dog" (Crick 1993, 123). Hampshire recognizes this when he observes of Rawls's political liberalism that it is "too gentle and too temperate in tone" (1993, 47) and that "adversarial politics scarcely enter into the argument" (44). As Hampshire notes, in Rawls's approach, we find "a very extended and substantial use of the words 'unreasonable' and 'public reason'" (44), but "the noise and muddle of actual politics are altogether absent, and history is scarcely called upon at all" (46). Regarding Habermas's approach, Michael Walzer has noted in a somewhat similar vein that, once Habermas's conditions for political discourse are met, those participating are seemingly "left with few substantive issues to argue and decide about. Social structure, political arrangements, distributive standards are pretty much given; there is room only for local adjustments" (Walzer 1994, 12).

To put the matter more bluntly, the preconditions that both Rawls and Habermas set for political discourse would seem to rule out of bounds much of what we ordinarily think of as politics. In contrast, Hampshire sets conditions for political discourse that are far more modest in character and that, as a result, allow for the practice of politics as we have come to understand it in the real world. According to Hampshire, what makes political "negotiation possible is not a set of shared first-order moral beliefs," but simply "a set of common practices" (1989, 188). As he expresses it, "persons of political experience, looking at each other fiercely across the table, are not required to respect each other as entire moral beings: only as reasonable in negotiation" (188). Furthermore, to be reasonable in political argumentation is not necessarily to make arguments "to which all possibly affected persons could assent as participants in rational discourses," as Habermas suggests. Nor does it require, as Rawls insists, that participants be "ready to explain their actions to one another in terms each could reasonably expect that others might endorse as consistent with their freedom and equality." To the contrary, to be reasonable in political argumentation, from Hampshire's perspective, is simply to be willing to hear the other side and to follow what have become locally accepted practices for the resolution of disputes. As he notes, "there is no rational necessity about the more specific rules and conventions determining the criteria for success in argument in any particular institution, except the overriding necessity that each side of the conflict should be heard putting its case" (2000, 18).

Moreover, as Hampshire makes clear, we should not overemphasize the importance of the particular beliefs that happen to be articulated in any particular political discourse. In fact, "articulate beliefs are secondary" because they are "supported by uncertain arguments and probable evidence and not by proofs, and therefore will not generally be agreed upon," and also because "where ideals are at issue, the particular passions and memories of the particular individuals involved will largely determine their beliefs" (Hampshire 1993, 46). From this pragmatic perspective, the "right reasons" or the "better arguments," therefore, are simply those that turn out to be persuasive to the various parties involved in helping them to resolve conflicts peacefully in a particular time and place.

In short, as Walzer argues, Hampshire is simply "not in the business of inventing or deducing ideal procedures to govern the argument and give shape and legitimacy to its outcomes" (1994, 14). Walzer explains that, from Hampshire's perspective, rather, "outcomes can be right or wrong, good or bad, in a more local and particularistic sense. What is important is that they be reached without tyrannical coercion or civil war" (14). In this regard, Hampshire's approach chimes well with Quentin Skinner's argument that, in moral and political debate, "our watchword ought to be *audi alteram partem,* always listen to the other side. This commitment stems from the belief that, in moral and political debate, it will always be possible to speak *in ultramque partem,* and will never be possible to couch our moral and political theories in deductive form. The appropriate model will always be that of a dialogue, the appropriate stance a willingness to negotiate over rival intuitions concerning the applicability of evaluative terms. We strive to reach understanding and resolve disputes in a conversational way" (1996, 15–16).

Hampshire's approach would also seem consistent with Rorty's belief that "one can only evaluate arguments by their efficacy in producing agreement among particular persons or groups" (2007, 54). From Rorty's perspective, like that of Hampshire, rationality is simply "what is present whenever people communicate, whenever they try to justify their claims to one another, rather than threatening each other" (51). As Rorty puts it, we should not think of reason "as a truth-tracking facility," but rather "as a social practice—the practice of enforcing social norms on the use of marks and noises, thereby making it possible to use words rather than blows as a way of getting things done" (107). Accordingly, when we tell people they should be rational, we are simply suggesting that, "somewhere among their shared beliefs and desires, there may be enough resources to permit agreement on how to coexist without violence" (53–54).

Of course, some may see as hopelessly naive Hampshire's view of politics as a means for resolving competing values or conceptions of the good by argument rather than by force. They might object that such processes of argumentation are no more than simply an elaborate and deceptive façade behind which competing groups exercise power to advance their narrow interests at the expense of others. However, while one cannot and should not ignore the role that interests play in politics, neither should one discount in politics the role of arguments and the sheer pleasure that we human beings seem to derive from engaging in them. As Hampshire points out, to view the reasons advanced in political argument as "always rationalizations," as just "mere decoration, designed to make the agent respectable in her own eyes and the eyes of others," is not really plausible because it "overlooks the active interest that men and women observably take both in the process and in the procedures of negotiation" (1989, 175–76). As he notes, human beings are, after all, among other things, "argumentative and litigious animals" who seem to take "delight in the rituals and procedures of argument, advocacy, and negotiation," so that "the various, and sometimes perverse, practices of law come naturally to them, no less than the various and perverse practices of sexuality" (176). According to Hampshire,

> Rhetoric has always engaged men's imaginations, and the desire to win an argument can be as intense as the desire to win a race. Most conspicuously in high politics, delight in the exercise of political skills in negotiation, and in the calculation of probable outcomes, often outweighs, or at least greatly complicates, an interest in the ultimate ends to be achieved. It is easy to underestimate the acute professional pleasure that politicians of sharply hostile purposes may take in their negotiations with each other and in the processes of manoeuvre and counter-manoeuvre. They recognize and respect in each other a passion and a pleasure, sometimes almost an addiction, which they do not share with the unpolitical mass of mankind. (176)

Procedural Justice and Constitutionalism

If we therefore accept, following Hampshire, that it is our historical practices of procedural justice or adversary argument, rather than any abstract principles, that can help us to resolve conflicts among competing moralities or conceptions of the good, then in thinking about how we might cope with these conflicts, it is quite reasonable for us—as either American writers or practitioners who are involved in public administration—to draw upon our own particular customary ideas and practices of procedural justice. Obviously, most prominent among these are the ideas and practices of American constitutionalism. James Madison himself clearly appreciated the dangers to a political community that were posed by clashes among different conceptions of the good. He worried about "the effects of the unsteadiness and injustice, with which a factious spirit has tainted our public administrations" (Wills 1982, 43). While it is quite true that Madison emphasized conflicts among economic interests or factions, he also fully understood and appreciated that conflicts could arise for other reasons. To use his words,

> A zeal for different opinions concerning religion, concerning Government and many other points, as well of speculation as of practice; an attachment to different leaders ambitiously contending for pre-eminence and power; or to persons of other descriptions whose fortunes have been interesting to the human passions, have in turn divided mankind into parties, inflamed them with mutual animosity, and rendered them much more disposed to vex and oppress each other, than to cooperate for their common good. So strong is this propensity of mankind to fall into mutual animosities, that where no substantial occasion presents itself, the most frivolous and fanciful distinctions have been sufficient to kindle their unfriendly passions, and excite their most violent conflicts. (44)

Furthermore, as we noted in chapter 3, the founders, in designing our particular constitution, deliberately sought through such means as an extended republic and a separation of powers what was essentially a series of veto points that would have the effect both of constraining the ability of any one group within government to impose its will by force upon others and of encouraging groups, as they sought their own particular ends through government, to accommodate themselves by means of politics to others seeking different ends. They made a point of emphasizing that they did not wish to rely solely upon written words or, as Madison put it, mere "parchment barriers" to protect citizens against "the encroaching spirit of power" (Wills 1982, 250). Rather, the founders sought to design a system of government such that its "constituent parts may, by their mutual relations, be the means of keeping each other in their proper place" (261). When viewed in terms of Hampshire's notion of procedural justice, our Constitution thus can be seen as checking the coercive power of government by providing multiple opportunities for settling conflicts among rival conceptions of the good through procedures of adversarial political argument in which different individuals and groups are given an opportunity to present their views on political disputes that affect them. Robert Dahl recognizes this important aspect of our constitutional form of governance when he argues that our system of governance "with all its defects, . . . does nonetheless provide a high probability that any active and legitimate group will make itself heard effectively at some stage in the process of decision" (1956, 150). As he notes, this is "no mean thing in a political system" (150). More recently, Richard Bellamy and Dario Castiglione have argued that the United States Constitution can usefully be seen as "a complex of institutions and conventions that facilitate . . . various styles of political dialogue . . . appropriate to the management of particular sorts of social and ideological conflict" (1997, 615). According to these authors, the founders made use of "a whole series of measures"—including the separation of powers, diverse voting systems for different representative bodies, and federalism—in order "to employ politics to achieve not only the traditional constitutional goal of checking arbitrary power, but also to secure informed, consensual and fair decision-making" (616). Their scheme involved "the creation of counter-balancing centres of decision making that devolve power up or down . . . in order to ensure that different values and interests get heard within the policy-making process" (616). That the founders themselves were quite conscious of providing exactly these types of opportunities for hearing the other side is evident, for example, in Madison's argument that a system of representative democracy would "refine and enlarge the public views" (Wills 1982, 46) and in Alexander Hamilton's observation that the advantage of a reasonably "numerous legislature" would be that "the differences of opinion, and the jarring of parties" would "promote deliberation and circumspection; and serve to check excesses in the majority" (358).

To appreciate more fully the role that our constitutional system of government plays in handling conflicts among different conceptions of the good, it is helpful to understand the origins of the liberal tradition of thought and practice from which it drew. In particular, these origins are to be found, in significant part, in the problems raised by religious conflicts, that is to say, conflicts over rival conceptions of the good, which often broke out into violence. Stephen Lukes recognizes this when he observes how "liberalism was born out of religious conflict and the attempt to tame it by accommodating it within the framework of the nation-state" (1989, 139). As Lukes notes, the argument for religious toleration was central to the development of liberalism, and "out of that there developed the crucial but complex thought that civil society is an arena of conflicts, which should be coordinated and regulated by the constitutional state" (139). Lukes readily concedes here that, in the development of liberal thought, it was recognized that social conflicts would result from "scarcity and conflicting claims that arise out of selfishness and competing interests" (139). However, as he argues, these conflicts were also seen as arising "more deeply, . . . out of conflicting moral claims," conflicting claims that raised "the problem of how to treat these justly within a framework of social unity and mutually accepted laws and principles of distribution" (139).

In light of the above, it follows, therefore, that the liberal ideas and practices of procedural justice that have evolved within our particular historical culture, while certainly not providing any guarantees of success at all, would seem especially well suited to the problem of resolving the type of conflicts among rival conceptions of the good that arise in our modern multicultural society and of protecting a broader range of such conceptions of the good than would be possible in their absence. They would seem to constitute exactly, to use Isaiah Berlin's words, the kind of "machinery designed to prevent people from doing each other too much harm, giving each human group sufficient room to realize its own idiosyncratic, unique, particular ends without too much interference with the ends of others" (Berlin 1992, 47).

Of course, to assert the value to us of such ideas and practices in dealing with our conflicting conceptions of the good is in no way to minimize the violence, the suffering, the atrocities that have sometimes occurred in the name of procedural justice and American constitutionalism, such as the protection of slavery and segregation and the mass relocation of native populations. Nor is it necessarily to condone more recent governmental practices such as high-tech surveillance of citizens without judicial warrants, long-term incarceration of terrorist suspects without trial, and interrogation techniques that, at the very least, seem to skirt the line with torture. As stressed above, no state, even one such as ours that emphasizes the norm of procedural justice, will achieve perfect fairness in the representation of conflicting moral outlooks. The institutions of procedural justice will often, if not always, be the result of past shabby political compromises. The best that can be expected is what Hampshire terms "a continuing approximation to contemporary ideals of fairness in resolving conflicts, and new institutions that tend to redress the more blatant inequalities" (2000, 32). In this regard, all we can claim perhaps is that, in comparison to monistic types of states, whether they be of the religious or secular variety, our historically contingent liberal state, by encouraging a process of continual adversarial argument among conflicting and incommensurable conceptions of the good, at the very least leaves more open for us the possibilities for continual change in our moral outlooks. In other words, by allowing conflict, our practices of procedural justice also allow for moral change. As Hampshire puts it, "That there should be a conflict between reflective desires, unreconciled outside an ideal world, is itself a condition of continuing moral development, both of the individual and of the species. If there is no valid theory to serve as the ground of a choice between irreconcilable dispositions, different choices will tend to be made by different men; and this vagary of choice will have an effect, being a form of experiment, in the development of the species" (1978, 44).

Politics, Constitutionalism, and Public Administration

What are the implications of this view of politics for public administration? Some might argue that we would be much better off and safer if public administrators simply left politics to their democratically elected political masters and followed the directives that are agreed upon by these masters. This was certainly the view of Max Weber, who, notwithstanding his concerns about bureaucracy, believed that, "according to his proper vocation, the genuine official . . . will not engage in politics," but rather should engage in "impartial administration" and that "the honor of the civil servant is vested in his ability to execute conscientiously the order of the superior authorities, exactly as if the order agreed with his own conviction" (1946, 95). Herman Finer also famously expressed such a view in a spirited debate with Carl Friedrich in the 1940s, when he wrote that "the servants of the public are not to decide their own course; they are to be responsible to the elected representatives of the public, and these are to determine the course of action of the public servants to the most minute degree that is technically feasible" (1941, 336). However, whatever our unease with the practice of politics in administration, the uncomfortable reality is that our constitutional form of politics makes the practice of a purely apolitical or instrumentalist approach to public administration very difficult, if not actually impossible. This is because power is highly dispersed and fragmented within our constitutional system so that, rather than following the directions of any one political leader or group of leaders, public administrators are able—and, in fact, in many cases find themselves compelled—to negotiate political support for their activities from a diverse set of political leaders and client groups. As a consequence, their activities are subject to the scrutiny, power, and influence of a multitude of different political actors, each of them advancing their own particular agendas and values (Long 1949; O'Neill 1988; Rohr 1986; Wilson 1989). As Norton Long made clear for us some sixty years ago, "the American system of government does not generate enough power at any focal point of leadership to provide the conditions for an even partially successful divorce of politics from administration," so that public administrators simply "cannot depend on the formal chain of command to deliver enough political power to permit them to do their jobs" (1949, 258). Rather, public administrators find themselves working within "a structure of interests friendly or hostile, vague and general or compact and well-defined," with power flowing "in from the sides of an organization" and also "up the organization to the center from the constituent parts" (258). Timothy O'Neill has argued similarly that the "forces fragmenting and diffusing political authority within and among the constitutionally described institutions of American government . . . compel the many American bureaucracies to build political support for their goals and programs" (1988, 390). As a result, we have what Dahl terms "a decentralized bargaining bureaucracy" (1956, 145), one in which public administrators bargain for support from other political actors and, as a result, cannot help but be intimately involved in the practice of politics. As Dahl succinctly expresses it, our bureaucracy "has become a part of . . . the 'normal' American political process" (145).

Because of our constitutional traditions, public administrators have inevitably been drawn into our political practices of procedural justice and have found themselves involved in situations that often require them, whether they like it or not, to hear the other side in administrative questions and, as a result, make choices among competing conceptions of the good. Public administration has become increasingly politicized, not in partisan terms so much, but rather in the sense that administrative decision making, in order to be effective, must be responsive to influence from a plurality of different and often conflicting interests and viewpoints within our system of governance. This is why, as O'Neill argues, "the language we use to describe bureaucratic policy-making—fragmented, disjointed, incremental, interest-group oriented—is similar to the language we use to describe the most accessible institution in the national government: the Congress" (1988, 391).

This politicization of public administration, which has its roots in our constitutional structure of governance, has had the effect of increasing the discretion available to administrators. As James Q. Wilson has argued, contrary to the economic models of agency theory popular nowadays among some contemporary political scientists and public management theorists, "Congress is almost never a 'principal' that can give unchallenged direction to its 'agent,' the bureaucracy" (1989, 237). Nor, for that matter, is bureaucracy the "helpless pawn of whatever control measures the president seeks to put in place" (274). Rather, the bureaucracy can "defer to the views of one part of the Congress (say, one committee) instead of another, or balance the competing demands of the White House with those of some parts of Congress in ways that other parts may not like" (237). According to Wilson, "the bureaucracy cannot evade political control nor sustain for long the view that there is a realm of 'administration' that is immune from 'politics.' But it can maneuver among its many political masters in ways that displease some of them and can define its tasks for internal reasons and not simply in response to external demands" (237).

This type of politicization of public administration has been further enhanced across the past six decades or so by the Administrative Procedure Act of 1946 and by subsequent legislation and court actions that have resulted in greater participation by different individuals, organizations, and groups in administrative decision making, as well as greater opportunities for them to mount administrative appeals and legal challenges to administrative actions (Rosenbloom 2000a, 2000b; Bingham, Nabatchi, and O'Leary 2005). The effect of these actions, as David Rosenbloom recently observed, is that our "administrative procedures now more closely reflect democratic-constitutional norms for legislating and governing in general" (Rosenbloom 2000a, 43). In Rosenbloom's view, these changes have produced what he terms a "legislative-centered public administration," one in which "Congress creates agencies, delegates legislative authority to them, and treats them as its extensions. It regulates their procedures, supervises them, and requires federal administration to comport with democratic-constitutional values as well as managerial ones" (2000b, 153–54). John Rohr has similarly observed that

> The legislative character of administration has become manifest in the participation, transparency, accountability, and protection of individual rights that infuse the American administrative process through such statutes as the Administrative Procedure Act, the Federal Advisory Committee Act, the Negotiated Rulemaking Act, and the Small Business Regulatory Fairness Enforcement Act, which encourage participation in rulemaking; the Freedom of Information Act and the Government in the Sunshine Act, which promote transparency; the Federal Tort Claims Act, which enhances accountability; and the Privacy Act and the adjudication sections of the Administrative Procedure Act, which protect individual rights. (2002, 83)

To look at this in another way, public administrators nowadays find themselves having to face multiple "forums of accountability," to use Udo Pesch's term (2005), so that the idea that public administrators should just go ahead and simply follow the directives of any single political master or single group of such masters, even if it was ever at all a credible idea, has now become increasingly fantastic. The fact that they are accountable to multiple forums obviously complicates the job of public administrators and can be frustrating for many of them. However, accountability to multiple forums can also help promote procedural justice in the practice of administration. This is because such accountability makes it more likely that administrators, as they attempt to garner political support for their actions and programs, will be compelled to hear and encouraged to take account of the different sides on issues that involve conflicts among different conceptions of the good. When they do so, fragmented and messy as it is, our decentralized and politicized administration gives public administrators the opportunity to exercise a significant measure of independent moral judgment in weighing competing values or conceptions of the good.

In contrast, the idea that public administrators should simply follow the directives of a single elected official or group of elected officials is not only impractical; it is also potentially harmful to the plurality of conflicting values that politics, as a process of hearing the other side, helps us to deal with. Of course, administrators should follow the law as enacted by their political superiors and as interpreted by the courts. However, it is far from clear that public administrators should allow themselves simply to serve as passive instruments to promote the particularistic ends or values promoted by any one particular group of elected political actors within our complex constitutional order. This is because such an approach to public administration is likely to give insufficient weight to the values held to be important by other groups in society, and thereby it risks a monist style of governance that could do damage to these values. An apolitical approach to public administration undermines the value of procedural justice in that it limits the ability of public administrators, in coming to a decision on an issue, to hear and take account of the views of different groups taking different positions on that issue. Therefore, as Peter French observes, it places the administrator in a "morally untenable position" because it asks the administrator "to relinquish his moral judgment and act as a machine, a slave . . . of the political executive who is his superior" (1983, 133). Consequently, this apolitical approach to public administration weakens any sense of moral responsibility that administrators have for their own actions. It encourages the type of bad faith, discussed in the previous chapter, where administrators pretend to others and to themselves that there is, to use Peter Berger's words, an "iron necessity" for "what they themselves are choosing to do" (1963, 144). In other words, an apolitical or instrumentalist approach to public administration undermines the moral responsibility of administrators.

It may be objected here that, notwithstanding these problems, an apolitical approach to public administration is nonetheless necessary for the proper functioning of democracy. However, when thinking about whether or not administrators should faithfully implement the directives of a particular elected official or group of officials, we would do well to remember, as noted earlier, that democracy is not the same thing as politics and to heed Berlin's warning that democracy can "crush individuals as mercilessly as any previous ruler" (1969, 163–64). As Berlin puts it, "democracy need not be pluralistic, it can be monistic, a democracy in which the majority does whatever it wants, no matter how cruel or unjust or irrational" (Berlin and Jahanbegloo 1991, 143–44). From a pluralist perspective, as Hampshire reminds us, "when a majority, following a natural tendency, advocates wrong policies—perhaps in the punishment of crime, in treatment of ethnic minorities, in immigration policy, in foreign policy, and elsewhere—the popularity of the policies cannot . . . mitigate the errors and the evil" (2000, 47). Viewed in this way, "the value of a democratic constitution lies in the defense of minorities, not of majorities" and "one needs to ensure, for the sake of justice, that the minorities are properly heard, and that they play their necessary part in the process" (47).

In this regard, notwithstanding the long debate in political philosophy about the meaning of democracy, there is perhaps much to recommend Karl Popper's view that democratic governments should be regarded simply as "governments of which we can get rid without bloodshed" (1966, 124). As Popper argues, when "seen in this light, . . . the various equalitarian methods of democratic control, such as general elections and representative government, are to be considered as no more than well-tried, . . . reasonably effective institutional safeguards against tyranny, always open to improvement, and even providing methods for their own improvement" (125). This view of democracy as a check on tyranny is consistent with James Madison's argument that a republic is "a government which derives all its powers directly or indirectly from the great body of the people; and is administered by persons holding their offices during pleasure, for a limited period, or during good behavior" (Wills 1982, 190). Such a view has the virtues, at least, of allowing democratic accountability without having to presume too much about the meaningfulness of any sort of democratic will, and also of being somewhat consistent with our constitutional traditions, including those of representative government and the separation of powers.

Implications

In light of the above discussion, the relevant question surely becomes not whether public administrators should or should not involve themselves in politics, but rather how they can do so in ways that would help to protect politics and value pluralism and to limit monist approaches to administrative action that do damage to values held to be important by different groups in society. Certainly, the foregoing discussion would seem to reinforce the critique, advanced in the previous chapter, of the type of science of governance that is offered by many public management writers. In particular, such a science of governance, rooted as it is in an instrumental rationalist perspective, offers little guidance to public administrators, who, in making decisions, find themselves having to respond to competing interests and moral claims within our system of governance. Indeed, if we accept that public administration is inevitably politicized in the specific sense in which I have used the term here, then perhaps the most important implication is that American public administrators should, as Rohr (1986) and others have emphasized, understand and respect our political and constitutional traditions of practice, and work within them. As David Rosenbloom, James Carroll, and Jonathan Carroll have rightly pointed out, public administrators should acquire "constitutional competence" because "constitutional government cannot function effectively without public management that embraces constitutional values" (2000, xvii). In acquiring and executing constitutional competence, public administrators not only can help themselves to stay out of court, but also make it more likely that different groups in society holding different and conflicting values will have an opportunity to have their views heard on administrative actions that affect them.

Beyond this, public administrators would do well to consider other ways to increase opportunities within their own agencies for hearing the other side on different administrative issues. One such approach, for example, is to actively recruit staff from a variety of different backgrounds and perspectives so as to encourage consideration of a broader range of points of view and values in administrative deliberations. Another approach would be for administrators to encourage their staff to express their viewpoints within the organization by creating, as Rosemary O'Leary puts it in her recent book, an "organizational culture that accepts, welcomes, and encourages candid dialogue and debate" and by cultivating "a questioning attitude by encouraging staff to challenge the assumptions and actions of the organization" (2006, 129). Moreover, the foregoing analysis would also indicate that there is merit in public administrators doing whatever they can to encourage the active participation in administrative decision making of those groups of citizens who are affected by their decisions. All of these approaches can be helpful in getting public administrators to hear the other side as they go about their business.

However, in accepting and even encouraging the practice of this type of politics in public administration, we should, at the same time, remain realistic in our expectations concerning what it is that politics can or, for that matter, should accomplish. We should remember, as discussed earlier in this chapter, that the practice of politics does not require any sort of deep moral consensus, but simply a willingness to resolve our differences using politics rather than force. In other words, we need to recognize that the "differing interests which create politics" cannot be "treated as a total moral and social unity" (Crick 1993, 127). It follows that public administrators should be careful, in dealing with other political actors, including citizens, not to assume or force a consensus where none exists and they should be attentive to the procedures that are used to structure political deliberation. This is especially true nowadays in light of the many different and conflicting conceptions of the good that arise in contemporary society. Different groups will sometimes, but not always, agree on actions to be taken and administrators should understand, as noted earlier, that what makes political negotiation possible is not any "set of shared first-order moral beliefs" but a "set of common practices" (Hampshire 1989, 188).

Furthermore, in thinking about the kind of discourse we wish to encourage, we should be careful, as discussed above, that we do not end up ruling out of bounds the conflict and passion that are characteristic of real-world politics. Rather than seeing political discourse ideally, as Habermas does, "as a regulated contest for better arguments based on the best information and reasons" (1998, 228), it may be more realistic, as well as more desirable, for public administrators to seek, more modestly, a discourse that simply provides for what is seen by participants as "a fair hearing to the two or more sides in a conflict" (Hampshire 2000, 55), a discourse that does not eliminate "the noise and muddle of actual politics," and one that allows for the expression of beliefs based on "the particular passions and memories" of those who are involved in conflicts with one another (Hampshire 1993, 46).

Moreover, we must also recognize that politics cannot and should not be concerned with the uncovering of a true "self" or some true common "social identity" that individuals have in common with others. To the contrary, as noted in chapter 3, the practice of politics presumes "some concern with personal identity" and with "its assertion and its preservation" (Crick 1993, 49), and so politics must "respect individuality, rather than try to dissolve it away" (127). To use Crick's words, "if man has a destiny, politics is obviously incompetent to legislate about it" and the best it can do is "to keep him alive and free to seek it" (152). Also, in light of the fact that citizens have many competing demands on their time, it is important to recognize that politics can "withstand a lot of apathy" (152). Indeed, as Crick reminds us, "when the normally apathetic person suddenly becomes greatly interested in political questions, it is often a sign of danger" (152). From this perspective, therefore, "politics should be praised for what it can do, but also praised for not attempting what it cannot do" (151).

In short, we should remember that the practice of politics, whether through citizen participation, elections, or other means, can never rid us of the conflicts that arise in our lives, both within us and between us, in regard to different values or conceptions of the good. We must recognize, to use Hampshire's words, that "life, and liveliness, within the soul and within society, consists in perpetual conflicts between rival impulses and ideals" (1989, 189) and that, while politics can help us deal with such conflicts, it can never dissolve them away. It is enough that politics, by providing opportunities for hearing the other side, can help us manage the conflicts that arise among us without too much violence and in a way that helps protect the plurality of conflicting values that, as argued in chapter 2, is an integral part of our moral experience as human beings.

6
Conclusion

Practical Moral Reasoning
in Public Administration

In this book, I have argued that our political practices, notwithstanding their limitations, serve to promote moral conduct by allowing us to resolve conflicts among values or rival conceptions of the good while avoiding the use of coercion. In the previous chapter, I argued that our historically situated institutions of politics help us to resolve value conflict in a nonviolent fashion because they provide opportunities for adversary argument or hearing the other side. In our particular system of constitutional government, one that makes the insulation of administration from politics often impossible, this means that public administrators have a responsibility to involve themselves in ways that help protect our political practices and value pluralism by preserving and enhancing these opportunities. It is in this way that politics in public administration can serve to promote moral conduct in government.

If this argument is correct, there are also other ways in which politics helps to promote moral conduct. In particular, our practices of politics may provide a basis for thinking about how public administrators, as individuals, might deal with situations they have to face involving value conflict. In this concluding chapter, I shall explore the role that a process of internal adversary argument, a process of adversary argument within the mind, can play in helping administrators to engage in practical moral reasoning. It must be admitted here that, notwithstanding the argument made so far that our political practices play an important role in the peaceful resolution of value conflict and in the protection of value pluralism, the idea that our practices of politics might actually provide guidance in moral reasoning to public administrators may strike some readers as a little odd. Nonetheless, as I shall argue, there are clear parallels between the way in which political institutions help us to resolve conflicts between competing conceptions of the good, and the way in which individuals themselves resolve these conflicts internally within their own minds. Specifically, the activity of practical moral reasoning shares with political practices a reliance on habits of adversary argument or hearing the other side. Finally, this chapter will explore how a more self-conscious cultivation of this process of practical moral reasoning, one that is derived from our social practices for resolving moral conflict, might be helpful to public administrators in both thinking about and dealing more effectively with conflicting ends or values. I argue here that public administrators can engage more effectively in this type of practical reasoning by drawing upon the type of rationality that is reflected in legal reasoning and upon the imaginative skills that can be provoked by reading literature and history.

In setting forth these arguments, I hope to show that while, as was argued in chapter 4, there is good reason to be critical of the type of science-based instrumental reasoning that is urged on us by public management writers, this does not mean that we have to abandon the use of human reasoning altogether when making choices among competing values. Of course, practical reasoning cannot—any more than instrumental reasoning—provide administrators any optimal solution to the problem of value conflict among incommensurable moral ends. However, practical reasoning can help administrators identify those situations in which such conflict occurs. Moreover, in doing so, it can encourage a consideration of a broader range of values in administrative decision making and thus reduce the likelihood that administrators in the pursuit of their particular missions or objectives will ignore values that we believe are important.

While advocating here for the use of this type of practical reasoning by public administrators, I should make it quite clear that I do not mean in any way to suggest that public administrators either can or should exercise unfettered discretionary power or ignore the legal and political checks that serve in our constitutional system of government to constrain their discretion. Nor would I argue that the exercise of such practical reasoning should somehow substitute for the type of political deliberations between public administrators and political leaders, citizens, interest groups, and fellow administrators discussed in the previous chapter. Public administrators in our constitutional form of government are not entitled and should never be encouraged to think of themselves as—or to act as if they were—philosopher kings. Rather, my point here is simply that, given what I have argued is the inevitably politicized character of American public administration, the exercise of practical reasoning by public administrators in regard to choices among conflicting values or conceptions of the good can usefully serve as a complement to the various political deliberations in which they either are or should be engaged.

Moral Reasoning and Adversary Reasoning

If we are to understand how public administrators should make decisions involving conflicting values, it is useful to begin by thinking about how we, as human beings in society, actually learn to engage in practical moral reasoning. Certainly most of us, at least if we are honest with ourselves, do not believe that we learn how to make moral choices by examining the works of moral philosophers, be they either of the deontological or utilitarian variety. Nor, for that matter, do we typically instruct our children in moral reasoning in this fashion, by having them read, for example, the works of Aristotle or Kant or Bentham. As Stuart Hampshire observes, the way that we learn how to reason about moral as well as other matters is not in a Cartesian manner as a result, as it were, of "solitary meditation by the stove" (2000, 11). Rather, we learn how to reason by observing and learning from, at an early stage in life, the various social institutions that we have come to use in adjudicating and deliberating about the various conflicts that arise among ourselves. In this respect, "mental processes in the minds of individuals" can be thought of as the "shadows" of "publicly identifiable procedures that are pervasive across different cultures" (7).

In other words, it is our local and diverse practices of procedural justice or adversary argument, practices that we have developed to avoid violence in the resolution of conflicts among our different conceptions of the good, that provide the model for the way in which we, as individuals, reason about moral matters. As Hampshire notes, "we learn to transfer, by a kind of mimicry, the adversarial pattern of public and interpersonal life onto a silent stage called the mind. The dialogues are internalized, but they still do not lose the marks of their origin in interpersonal adversarial argument. Viewed in this way, the mind is the unseen and imagined forum into which we learn to project the visible and audible social processes that we first encounter in childhood: practices of asserting, contradicting, deciding, predicting, recalling, approving and disapproving, admiring, blaming, rejecting and accepting, and many more" (2000, 11–12).

The fact that our moral reasoning is rooted in our social practices helps to explain why so many of the words that we typically use in thinking or talking about making moral choices—words such as "deliberating," "judging," "reviewing," "adjudicating" and "examining"—are appropriated from the various social procedures that we use to adjudicate conflicts between different individuals and groups in society. Such words have "both a public and an inner mental use" (Hampshire 2000, 7). As Hampshire argues,

> We have to borrow the vocabulary that is to describe the operations of our
> minds from the vocabulary that describes the public and observable trans-

actions of social life. The picture of the mind that gives substance to the notion of practical reason is a picture of a council chamber, in which the agent's contrary interests are represented around the table, each speaking for itself. The chairman, who represents the will, weighs the arguments and the intensity of the feeling conveyed by the arguments, and then issues an order to be acted on. The order is a decision and an intention, to be followed by its execution. The policy is the outcome of the debate in the council chamber. (1989, 51)

Moreover, as Hampshire points out, just as "in the council chamber, there is the reasonable requirement of fairness in attending to the arguments from all sides of the council chamber, of minimum procedural justice," so there is also within our minds "a corresponding judiciousness in any internal debate, where this habit of fairness amounts to practical wisdom" (1989, 94). In other words, whenever we engage in practical reasoning concerning moral matters, we draw upon habits of thinking about procedural justice or fairness that we have picked up in seeking to resolve interpersonal or social conflicts that have arisen among ourselves. As Hampshire observes, "the idea of an individual's being unbiased, open-minded, and rational in his thinking has sense for us because we know what it is for a public procedure of discussion to be unbiased, open-minded, and rational. I imagine myself hearing two or more contrary cases presented to me, and I preside over them, allowing the evidence on both sides to be heard; then, and only then, I am to reach a conclusion. This is the process of reflection" (2000, 10–11).

Furthermore, it should be emphasized that, once these habits of practical reasoning have become internalized, such habits in turn serve to facilitate and to foster engagement by men and women in social processes of adversary reasoning. In other words, while our mental habits of practical reasoning have their roots in our social practices of procedural justice, once engendered in our minds, they also act in turn to reinforce our social practices. As Hampshire argues, it is because "at first hand, we know about the reflective balancing of pros and cons from which we have to construct some degree of consistency in action and in attitude for ourselves" that "we can recognize and respond to the contraries of political debate and public argument" (2000, 72). In this sense, "a minimum of decent fairness, both in personal relations and in public affairs . . . is rooted in the fact that humans have to some degree the habit of balancing contrary arguments and drawing conclusions from them" (Hampshire 1989, 169). Hampshire notes here how, even among political opponents, "everyone has adversaries within his own soul and is in this way already prepared to step out onto the political or legal stage and to argue his case. He has already rehearsed the fairness of a statement followed by a rebuttal, followed by a restatement in his own thinking. If he and his adversary abstain from force, they both know the rational procedure that remains" (2000, 93–94). It is for this reason that, as Hampshire points out, "procedural justice is supported by the impulses and the temperament which create lawyers and orators, who instinctively see power as persuasion rather than as conquest, and who cultivate and enjoy the skills of bargaining and of debate" (Hampshire 1989, 176). Thus, our mental habits of practical reasoning both are derived from and promote our engagement in social practices of adversarial argument and procedural justice.

If the foregoing argument is accepted, then it follows that a more self-conscious exercise of practical reasoning in public administration might serve to protect value pluralism much better than the science-based instrumental rationalism that, as we have seen, pervades so much of our field. This is because, by encouraging an internal deliberative process of hearing both sides of a dispute, a more self-conscious exercise of practical reasoning can remind administrators of the reality of the moral conflicts that they face and thereby can act as a check on the overly zealous pursuit by administrators of one particular set of values at the expense of others. Furthermore, the development of habits of practical reasoning among administrators can help to protect value pluralism by fostering their engagement in processes of adversary argument rather than domination or violence.

Legal Reasoning as Adversary Reasoning

If we accept that to exercise practical reason in making decisions among competing ends means to engage in a process of internal adversary argument, what are the implications of this for public administration? First, in my view, we would do well to expose our students much more than we typically have to the process of legal or juridical reasoning. This is, of course, in no way to claim that moral reasoning is the same as legal reasoning. Rather, it is simply to suggest that we can learn something useful about moral reasoning from legal reasoning. After all, it is law, as a practice, that provides the most self-conscious and formal expression of the norm of procedural justice, *audi alteram partem,* a norm that, as we have seen, characterizes practical moral reasoning. As Chaïm Perelman has observed, in law, unlike in geometry or formal logic, "we admit that two reasonable and honest men can disagree on a determined question and thus judge differently. The situation is . . . considered so normal, both in legislative assemblies and in tribunals that have several judges, that decisions made unanimously are esteemed exceptional; and it is normal, moreover, to provide for procedures permitting the reaching of decisions even when opposing opinions persist" (1980, 165).

Furthermore, according to Perelman, in law we accept "the notion of a decision which, even if not rational in the sense of its conformity with formal deduction, should be reasonable, or at least reasoned" (1980, 166). Law involves a process of reasoning in which an argument for a particular legal rule "does not in any way constitute a deduction, and the conclusion which it reaches is in no way constraining" (170–71). Rather, "the reasons in favor of [a particular] rule are arguments of greater or lesser strength to which reasons in an adverse sense, themselves arguments of greater or lesser strength, can normally be opposed" (171). This is why, to use Perelman's words, "the law is essentially pluralistic. It lives to realize many values simultaneously and can, in concrete situations, protect incompatible ones. Those will carry the day which seem the best in the eyes of the judge and for which we have presented the best reasons" (160). This occurs despite the fact that, as Perelman notes, "the force of these reasons cannot be measured or weighed" (160).

The parallels here between legal reasoning and practical moral reasoning are striking and, indeed, Perelman himself observes how "ratiocination about values is much more like a juridical argument than like a mathematical deduction" (1955, 798). Such parallels should not be surprising given that, as noted above, we learn how to reason in moral matters not by solitary meditation but rather by observing the institutional processes that we use to resolve conflict among ourselves, including those of the courts. As Hampshire observes, anyone who participates in a "law court," as well as other forms of "public adversarial discussions, . . . acquires the habit of preparing for rebuttals by opponents. He acquires the habit of balanced adversary thinking" (2000, 9). It follows, therefore, that familiarity with legal reasoning would be helpful to public administrators in dealing with conflicts among rival values or conceptions of the good. In this respect, I agree with John Rohr when he suggests that, by reading Supreme Court opinions, for example, students of public administration might become more sensitive to the "many conflicting interpretations of American values" that have existed and continue to exist within our society (1976, 404). According to Rohr, "the presence of concurring and dissenting opinions in Supreme Court decisions" offers those who wish to practice public administration "alternative ways of looking at the same problem" and can thus help them to "avoid the danger of accepting dogmatic assertions uncritically" (403).

Legal Reasoning as Analogical Reasoning

Moreover, exposure of public administrators to legal reasoning is useful not simply because it is rooted in the idea of resolving conflict among values by means of adversary argument. It is also useful because an important characteristic of legal reasoning, especially in Anglo-American law, is its reliance upon the practice of argument by analogy or example. In fact, legal reasoning in many ways represents the paradigmatic form of what has been termed "analogical reasoning." Edward Levi recognized this over a half century ago, when he wrote that "the basic pattern of legal reasoning is reasoning by example. It is reasoning from case to case. It is a three-step process described by the doctrine of precedent in which a proposition descriptive of the first case is made into a rule of law and then applied to a next similar situation. The steps are these: similarity is seen between cases: next, the rule of law in the first case is announced, then the rule is made applicable to the second case" (1949, 1–2).

Hilliard Aronovich has argued more recently that it is within law that the role of analogical reasoning is "most readily recognized and commonly accepted" (1997, 82). Aronovich defines analogical reasoning as "reasoning from case to case, by example or paradigm instance, whereby it is inferred that a characteristic of an established case should apply to a novel, similar one" (79). Its object, according to Aronovich, is "to draw lessons from the past by way of specially selected particulars," and it results in arguments that may be judged as "relatively and not definitively persuasive or unpersuasive, as providing support for the conclusion that is anywhere from overwhelmingly strong to uselessly weak, and most often somewhere in between" (79–80). Generally speaking, while analogical arguments can never be proven demonstrably to be correct or incorrect, "the more there are specific and relevant respects of likeness in the initial analogy, the better the argument on the whole will be, . . . the fewer the relevant and significant disanalogies or differences between the familiar and the unfamiliar entities, the better for the argument" (81).

Of course, analogical reasoning is not without its critics (see, for example, Alexander 1996). Even Cass Sunstein, who is clearly sympathetic to the use of analogical reasoning in law, concedes that it cannot "guarantee good outcomes or truth" (1993, 745). As he notes, "the major challenge facing analogical reasoners is to decide when differences are relevant" (745), and analogical reasoning can go seriously astray "when there is an inadequate inquiry into the matter of relevant differences and governing principles" (746). Notwithstanding these limitations, however, analogical reasoning can assist public administrators in resolving conflicts that arise among incommensurable moral claims or values. This is because it can help provide a reasoned justification for decisions that have to be made in a particular case or situation without the necessity of providing for any sort of universal or definitive ranking of those claims.

Reasoned justification, even when incommensurable moral claims are in conflict with one another, is especially important in public administration since, as public officials, public administrators are held accountable for the decisions that they make, and therefore they are obliged and must be prepared to defend publicly these decisions on grounds that they hope will seem reasonable both to their superiors and to the public. As Hampshire argues, in public morality as distinguished from private morality, "there is a greater requirement of explicitness of reasoning" in that the public official is expected to be able "to give an account of the reasons for his policies" (1983, 122). In defending public actions, "appeals to intuitions of right and wrong will usually not be an adequate defense" (122). Mary Warnock argues similarly that, "in the sphere of public morality, it is not enough for a public official simply to say, 'I feel I must' do this or that" (2004, 25). Rather, those who are involved in public life "owe a duty to be able to explain why they have come to the conclusion they have. They must be seen to have thought rationally" (25).

Analogical reasoning, as a particular form of reasoning, fits well with value pluralism because it allows for the possibility that reasoned arguments often may be asserted on either side of a moral or political question. In fact, as Aronovich observes, on occasion "opposed analogical arguments on an issue may each be persuasive in about equal measure" (1997, 80). This form of reasoning is appropriate in cases where values or moral claims are incommensurable with one another, because, in such cases, arguments for different conceptions of the good may each be, as George Crowder notes, "prima facie reasonable, and many will be equally reasonable" so that "many disagreements concerning the merits of rival conceptions of the good will also be reasonable" (2004, 159).

Moreover, analogical reasoning would seem especially helpful in dealing with value conflict because, in examining the similarities as well as the differences between specific cases or examples, analogical reasoning is sensitive to the details of the situation in which choices among conflicting values must be made. As Sunstein notes, "analogical reasoning focuses on particulars, and it develops from concrete controversies. . . . Ideas are developed from the details, rather than imposed on them from above" (1993, 746). In other words, analogical reasoning draws the attention of the decision maker to the context in which moral choices are made. This attention to context is important because, when making choices among conflicting values, as Isaiah Berlin reminds us, "the concrete situation is almost everything" (1992, 18). By paying attention to context, analogical thinkers are more likely to be aware of value conflicts where they occur. As Sunstein puts it, "The analogical thinker is alert to the manifold dimensions of social situations and to multiple relevant similarities and differences. Unequipped with (or unburdened by) a unitary theory of the good or the right, she is in a position to see clearly . . . the diverse and plural goods that are at stake and to make choices among them. The very search for relevant similarities and differences places a premium on this process of perceiving particulars" (1993, 789).

As a result, those who use analogical reasoning are less likely to feel compelled to apply general principles in those cases where they simply do not fit. Rather, as Sunstein argues, analogical thinkers are "peculiarly alert to the inconsistent or abhorrent result, and they take strong convictions about particular cases to provide reasons for reevaluating their views about other cases or even about apparently guiding general principles" (1993, 791). Because of this willingness to reevaluate their general principles in light of particular cases when appropriate, analogical thinkers, while not immune from, are more likely to avoid the "fanaticism in law and politics" that comes from an "insistence on applying general principles to particular cases" even where this produces "palpable absurdity or palpable injustice" (750).

In light of the above, a good argument can be made that public administrators, faced with making choices among conflicting conceptions of the good, should make greater use of the type of analogical reasoning that is employed in legal reasoning. At the very least, when compared with the instrumental reasoning characteristic of conventional social science, analogical reasoning makes it more likely that conflicts among different values or moral claims will be considered when making decisions. Unlike the former, analogical reasoning, in order to make itself useful, need not, to use Sunstein's words, "insist that plural and diverse social goods should be assessed according to the same metric" (1993, 788).

Furthermore, the use of analogical reasoning would seem appropriate to public administration, if only because it has always been pervasive in all kinds of political discourse dating back at least to ancient Greece. Hampshire sees this when he notes how, in political discussions about justice, arguments supporting contrary claims are typically "drawn from moral assumptions and approved practices which have to some extent prevailed hitherto" (1989, 63). As he puts it, "In any political system that is designed to eliminate or to lessen a particular injustice, public argument will revolve around the plausible analogies between the disputed case and cases of injustice in the same or a similar domain" (2000, 63). "The arguments proceed by a kind of appeal to accepted cases of injustice: Can you not see that having slaves is unjust, because it entails treating people as if they were domestic animals, and as not fully human? Will you not see that factory labour, left unregulated, is in effect like slave labour, when the workers have only their labour to sell? Will you not see that women, no less than men, are capable of useful work and of thought, of discovery and of creation, and that it is unjust that they should not have equal opportunities?" (Hampshire 1989, 63). Of course, such analogical arguments in politics, as in the law, can never be shown to be demonstrably correct and are open to contestation. As Hampshire notes, they "will not have anything like the form of a logical demonstration and will not exhibit the rigor of a proof in mathematics. As is characteristic of moral and political and legal arguments, they will be citing evidence and reasons that incline without necessitating" (2000, 63–64).

Aronovich similarly observes that "a great deal of actual political debate" takes "the form of claiming: this is like that (event, person, decision, etc.) and we wish to imitate or avoid that, and hence we should do or refrain from this" (1997, 87). He also notes that the lessons to be learned from particular analogies or precedents may be open to quite different interpretations. Aronovich asks us to "consider the power, in the US and elsewhere, of the phrase 'No more Vietnams!' as a way of warning against a whole range of involvements. The fact that it can be subject to quite opposite intentions and meanings ('Next time, fight to win!' versus 'Avoid such entanglements altogether') shows vividly that interpretation of precedents is the essence of events as precedents" (87).

Given this ubiquity of reasoning by analogy in politics, as well as its particular usefulness in dealing with issues involving multiple values, it is reasonable, therefore, to suggest that public administrators seeking guidance in practical moral reasoning might profit by examining its application within the context of law. This argument is made more plausible by Jay White's argument that many public administrators, in fact, already use this type of reasoning in reaching decisions. As White notes, "Administrators are in the same place as lawyers and judges. They go beyond the limits of instrumental reasoning to employ reasoning by example . . . to determine what ends should be sought and what actions should be taken. Like lawyers and judges they are in the business of making choices about what is true or false, good or bad. Experience suggests that this is done on the basis of reasoning by example. Since administrators and judges (or lawyers) are human beings, there is no a priori reason to believe that their reasoning processes are any different: only the contexts differ" (1990, 138).

"Firing the Imagination"

However, while legal reasoning can be helpful to public administrators, as our own tainted judicial history unfortunately makes only too clear, legal reasoning alone cannot provide a sufficient guide for moral action in public administration or, for that matter, in our ordinary lives. Moral reasoning is similar to legal reasoning, but, as noted above, it is not the same as legal reasoning. According to Hampshire, one important difference "between a moral, and a merely legal, argument around a conflict of claims" is "that imagination will not be called for in legal argument as it often will be in moral contexts" (1983, 30). Hampshire's characterization of legal argument as devoid of imagination may strike some here as overly simplistic, as well as perhaps a little insulting to lawyers. Nevertheless, it is probably true that moral reasoning calls for a greater degree of imagination than is typically found in legal reasoning. This is because legal reasoning proceeds on the basis of explicit evidence and arguments presented by opposing parties in a case, whereas persons engaged in moral reasoning can draw only upon those pieces of evidence and arguments they are either able or choose to bring to mind. It is in this process of "bringing to mind" that human imagination plays a significant role. Hampshire recognizes the role that imagination plays in practical reasoning when he notes that, "from the standpoint of an individual, rationality and fairness in procedure is the habit of examining particular conflicts and their precedents by imagining oneself changing one's role within the process" (2000, 71). Moreover, he acknowledges, at least implicitly, the particular importance of imagination in the use of practical reasoning in government when he observes that, whenever "a politician weighs two moral claims on him, . . . the basic decency, the universal requirement, is that the politician should establish the nature of the claims upon him *in their own terms* before he restates them in his own terms" (1989, 187; italics added).

Imagination in practical moral reasoning is important because, as Richard Rorty observes, in discussing the relationship between reason and imagination, "reason can only follow the paths that the imagination has broken, only rearrange the paths that the imagination has created" (2007, 112). For Rorty, what we like to call rationality is "a matter of making allowed moves within language games," but it is imagination that "creates the games that reason proceeds to play" and "keeps modifying those games so that playing them is more interesting and profitable" (115). Consequently, "reason cannot get outside the latest circle that imagination has drawn" (115). It is in this sense that "imagination has priority over reason" (115).

If this is correct, then, public administrators might be usefully encouraged to adopt a form of what Robert Goodin has called "internal-reflective" deliberation (2000, 81). Concerned about what he sees as the many obstacles to deliberative democracy within a large modern state, Goodin has argued that we need to "ease the burdens of deliberative democracy in mass society by altering our focus from the 'external collective' to the 'internal reflective' mode, shifting much of the work of democratic deliberation back inside the head of each individual" (83). By this he means that we need to encourage citizens, in reasoning about public issues, to self-consciously imagine a discourse on these issues among different people taking different positions, a process of "empathetic imagining" or "making others imaginatively present" (83–84). Goodin appears to believe that all of us as citizens generally should be encouraged to engage in this type of empathetic imagining as a way of overcoming the limitations of deliberative democracy in modern society. According to Goodin, this kind of "empathetic imagining can be an important supplement to . . . interpersonal conversation in the sorts of deliberations that democrats desire across mass societies" (83). As he notes, "through the exercise of a suitably informed imagination, each of us might be able to conduct a wide-ranging debate within our own heads among all the contending perspectives" (98).

Such empathetic imagining would seem to fit well with the plurality of ends or conceptions of the good that is characteristic of politics. As Hannah Arendt once wrote, "Political thought is representative. I form an opinion by considering a given issue from different viewpoints, by making present to my mind the standpoints of those who are absent; that is, I represent them. . . . The more people's standpoints I have present in my mind while I am pondering a given issue, and the better I can imagine how I would feel and think if I were in their place, the stronger will be my capacity for representative thinking" (2000, 556).

Admittedly, the idea of large numbers of citizens engaging in such imaginative internal deliberation appears more than a little fanciful, especially given the limitations on time and information that most citizens, already busy with their hectic lives, are faced with. However, surely it is far less fanciful to suggest that this is precisely how public administrators might attempt to deal with particular political issues that they already have to face. Indeed, public administrators arguably have a special moral responsibility to engage in internal reflective deliberation. This is because they have greater access to information about public issues, they are paid for their time, and they are able to wield considerable power over the lives of their fellow citizens. If this is true, the question therefore arises as to how we might best encourage public administrators to exercise their imaginations in this fashion, how we might encourage, to use Goodin's words, a process of "firing the imagination" (2000, 95).

Goodin argues here that exposure to artistic works such as novels can serve such a function. As Goodin sees it, novelists can stimulate our imaginations because "they fix their focus on the particular—one person or one action or one period—and they introduce generalities by way of anecdotes, episodes viewed from that particular perspective. That vivid evocation of the particular, in turn, has important consequences for the uptake of works of art. Inevitably, we find it relatively easy to imagine ourselves into the place of some specific (fictitious but grounded) other" (2000, 96). James Harold notes similarly how the reading of fiction can help "contribute to the improvement of the moral imagination" by helping us to "imagine what it is like to be another" (2003, 255). According to him, such "fictive imagining . . . can help us to better understand one another, and to better appreciate just how much there is to understand about others" (255).

The foregoing is consistent with Rorty's argument that literature offers us "re-

demption through making the acquaintance of as great a variety of human beings as possible" (2007, 91). As Rorty puts it, "the more books you have read, the
more ways of being human you have considered, the more human you become—
the less tempted by dreams of an escape from time and chance, the more con-
vinced that we humans have nothing to rely on save one another" (95).

By extending our imagination, literature can help us avoid the type of bad
faith discussed in chapter 4, which arises in public administration when we pretend to ourselves that "something is necessary that is in fact voluntary" (Berger
1963, 143). It can help to curb what Michael Oakeshott terms our "craving for
demonstrative political argument" (1991, 95) by reminding us of the reality of
the moral choices that are, in fact, open to us, and the heavy responsibility that
these choices place upon us. As Hampshire observes, when we follow "an imaginative story on stage, or in a novel, we recapture the sense of uncertainty and of
open possibilities which we experience in actual living. We are introduced by the
author to the missed possibilities on the margins of the actual events supposed,
because dramatists can create their own space of possibilities, as painters create
their own space within a picture" (1989, 105).

Unlike social science, literature, by inspiring our imagination, can draw our
attention to the moral complexities and conflicts that practical moral reasoning
must deal with. As Bernard Crick argues, "the very form of the novel arises
from and embraces conflicts of character, values, interests, circumstances and
classes" (1989, 17). "Where else," he asks, "can one look to for graphic portrayals
of moral dilemmas in general and of conflicts of ethical principle and political
prudence?" (17). Hilary Putnam observes likewise how the novel can aid us "in
the imaginative re-creation of moral perplexities in the broadest sense" (1976,
485). Exposure to various types of literature, as well as nowadays of course, dra-
matic films and even television dramas, can thus assist public administrators in
the process of practical reasoning in moral affairs by making more real or vivid
the views of different sides in the moral disputes that they are called upon to resolve. Equally important, it can help alert them to value conflicts that are already
implicit in the choices that they are making, but that would otherwise remain
hidden or invisible to them.

Finally, history—at least where it pays attention to the concrete details of
human experience in different times rather than speculating abstractly about
broad historical forces, as it is sometimes prone to—can also play a role in stimu-
lating the imaginations of public administrators and in encouraging an understanding of different conceptions of the good. As Berlin argues, the task of the
historian is "reconstructing what occurred in the past in terms not merely of our
own concepts and categories, but also of how such events must have looked to
those who participated in or were affected by them—psychological facts that

in turn themselves influenced events" (1979, 135). This involves "an imaginative projection of ourselves into the past, the attempt to capture concepts and categories that differ from those of the investigator by means of concepts and categories that cannot but be his own. . . . We cannot evade the task of interpretation, for nothing counts as a historical interpretation unless it attempts to answer the question of how the world must have looked to other individuals or societies if their acts and words are to be taken as the acts and words of human beings neither wholly like ourselves nor so different as not to fit into our common past" (135–36). Historians, when they do their job well, exercise what Berlin calls "imaginative insight," a skill in bringing before us a "revelation of a form of life, . . . in bringing a past age to life" (1996, 25). As Raphael Demos recognized some four decades ago, "at its best, history fuses scholarship with the literary imagination . . . so that the reader may live through and experience the past, faithfully recorded" (1969, 298). According to Demos, the historian "produces the illusion of presentness—the quality of immediacy which the past had when it was a present fact—and this he does by literary evocation. . . . In history, . . . we try to remember the dead as they were when they were still alive" (298). In doing so, like novelists and dramatists, historians can fire our imaginations by allowing us to conceive of human beings with values or conceptions of the good, some of which are familiar, some of which are strange and some of which conflict with those that we happen to hold. It is in this way that an exposure to history can help public administrators in the exercise of practical reasoning about moral matters.

Conclusion

In summary, public administrators can engage more effectively in practical moral reasoning by drawing upon the kind of adversary and analogical reasoning that is used within law and upon the kind of imaginative skills that are brought into play in reading literature and history. In drawing upon these different ways of thinking, public administrators can become more aware of the inevitability of value conflict in the decisions they are called upon to make and, as a result, be more likely to deal with it in a way that protects the variety of moral ends that we have come to regard as important to us. Of course, it must be emphasized that exposure to legal reasoning, literature, and history cannot alone assure that the decisions of public administrators will deal fairly with competing conceptions of the good. The various political and legal institutions of procedural justice discussed in the previous chapter, including those provided by our Constitution, have played and must continue to play a critical role in extending the range of values that public administrators must respond to and also in limiting any monist inclinations that they, or those directly supervising their activities, might have. Moreover, as already noted, there is much to recommend the idea that public administrators should think about ways in which processes of procedural justice, or opportunities for hearing the other side, can be fostered and promoted both within their organizations and in their dealings with citizens. My only point here is that public administrators can also assist in this process by engaging more self-consciously in a type of practical reasoning that more closely mirrors the adversarial character of these institutions. In doing so, public administrators can internalize the spirit and logic of the checks and balances that are characteristic of our particular brand of constitutional politics.

If nothing else, greater exposure to law, literature, and history can alert us in public administration to the fact that, whatever our own particular conceptions of the good happen to be, conflict in society is not an aberration or, as Hampshire terms it, "the sign of a vice, or a defect, or a malfunctioning," or "a deviation from the normal state of a city or of a nation," or "a deviation from the normal course of the person's experience" (2000, 33). These fields of human thought remind us, rather, that conflict is something quite normal and that there is virtue in seeking to resolve such conflict by political practices of adversarial argument rather than violence. Conflict is normal not simply, as we are so often reminded, because of human weaknesses, but also because of the varieties of different conceptions of the good that we, as human beings in different circumstances, seem capable of imagining. An awareness of the normality of conflict is important since so much of our field, as I have argued in this book, expresses a science-based instrumental rationalist mindset that constantly draws our attention towards questions about how best to pursue given ends but, in doing so, draws our attention away from important questions about how to reconcile our conflicting and incommensurable ends. Law, literature, and history, with their attention to human conflict in particular concrete circumstances, serve to remind us that "we should look in society not for consensus, but for ineliminable and acceptable conflicts, and for rationally controlled hostilities, as the normal condition of mankind; not only normal, but also the best condition of mankind from the moral point of view, both between states and within states" (Hampshire 1989, 189). As Hampshire points out, "conflict is perpetual: why then should we be deceived?" (2000, 48). By embracing this idea that moral conflict is inevitable, we can develop a better understanding of, and an appreciation for, the character of politics and the crucial role that it plays in fostering moral conduct.

References

Alexander, Larry. 1996. "Bad Beginnings." *University of Pennsylvania Law Review* 145:57–87.

Almond, Gabriel A., and Stephen J. Genco. 1977. "Clouds, Clocks, and the Study of Politics." *World Politics* 29:489–522.

Archard, David, ed. 1996. *Philosophy and Pluralism.* Cambridge: Cambridge University Press.

Arendt, Hannah. 2000. *The Portable Hannah Arendt.* Ed. Peter Baehr. New York: Penguin Books.

Aristotle. 1946. *The Politics of Aristotle.* Trans. Ernest Barker. Oxford: Clarendon Press.

———. 1999. *Nicomachean Ethics.* 2nd ed. Trans. Terence Irwin. Indianapolis: Hackett Publishing.

Aronovich, Hilliard. 1997. "The Political Importance of Analogical Argument." *Political Studies* 45:78–92.

Babbie, Earl R. 1975. *The Practice of Social Research.* Belmont, CA: Wadsworth Publishing.

———. 1986. *Observing Ourselves: Essays in Social Research.* Belmont, CA: Wadsworth Publishing.

Bailey, Stephen K. 1964. "Ethics and the Public Service." *Public Administration Review* 24:234–43.

Bailyn, Bernard. 2003. *To Begin the World Anew: The Genius and Ambiguities of the American Founders.* New York: Alfred A. Knopf.

Behn, Robert. 1998. "What Right Do Public Managers Have to Lead?" *Public Administration Review* 58:209–24.

Bellamy, Richard. 2000. "Dealing with Difference: Four Models of Pluralist Politics." *Parliamentary Affairs* 53:198–217.

Bellamy, Richard, and Dario Castiglione. 1997. "Constitutionalism and Democracy—Political Theory and the American Constitution." *British Journal of Political Science* 27:595–618.

Berger, Peter L. 1963. *Invitation to Sociology: A Humanistic Perspective.* New York: Doubleday.

Berlin, Isaiah. 1969. *Four Essays on Liberty.* New York: Oxford University Press.

———. 1979. *Concepts and Categories: Philosophical Essays.* New York: Viking Press.

———. 1982. *Against the Current: Essays in the History of Ideas.* New York: Penguin Books.

———. 1992. *The Crooked Timber of Humanity: Chapters in the History of Ideas.* New York: Vintage Books.

———. 1996. *The Sense of Reality: Studies in Ideas and Their History.* New York: Farrar, Straus and Giroux.

———. 2000. *The Power of Ideas.* Princeton, NJ: Princeton University Press.

Berlin, Isaiah, and Ramin Jahanbegloo. 1991. *Conversations with Isaiah Berlin.* New York: Charles Scribner's Sons.

Bingham, Lisa Blomgren, Tina Nabatchi, and Rosemary O'Leary. 2005. "The New Governance: Practices and Processes for Stakeholder and Citizen Participation in the Work of Government." *Public Administration Review* 65:547–58.

Bogason, Peter, Melvin J. Dubnick, John J. Kirlin, Kenneth J. Meier, Janet Foley Orosz, Jos C. N. Raadschelders, and Curt Ventriss. 2000. "Dialogue: Knowledge and Research." *Administrative Theory and Praxis* 22:393–423.

Box, Richard. 1992. "An Examination of the Debate over Research in Public Administration." *Public Administration Review* 52:62–69.

Caiden, Gerald E. 1984. "In Search of an Apolitical Science of American Public Administration." In *Politics and Administration: Woodrow Wilson and American Public Administration,* ed. Jack Rabin and James S. Bowman. New York: Marcel Dekker.

Crick, Bernard. 1989. *Essays on Politics and Literature.* Edinburgh: Edinburgh University Press.

———. [1962] 1993. *In Defence of Politics.* 4th ed. Chicago: University of Chicago Press.

Crowder, George. 1994. "Pluralism and Liberalism." *Political Studies* 42:293–305.

———. 2004. *Isaiah Berlin: Liberty and Pluralism.* Cambridge: Polity Press.

Dahl, Robert A. 1956. *A Preface to Democratic Theory.* Chicago: University of Chicago Press.

Daneke, Gregory A. 2005. "The Reluctant Resurrection: New Complexity Methods and Old Systems Theories." *International Journal of Public Administration* 28: 89–106.

Deese, James. 1985. *American Freedom and the Social Sciences.* New York: Columbia University Press.

deLeon, Peter. 1992. "The Democratization of the Policy Sciences." *Public Administration Review* 52:125–34.

Demos, Raphael. 1969. "The Language of History." In vol. 2 of *Ideas of History,* ed. Ronald H. Nash. New York: E. P. Dutton.

Denhardt, Robert B. 1981. "Toward a Critical Theory of Public Organization." *Public Administration Review* 41:628–35.

———. 2000. *Theories of Public Organization.* 3rd ed. Fort Worth, TX: Harcourt Brace.

Easton, David. 1953. *The Political System: An Inquiry into the State of Political Science.* New York: Alfred A. Knopf.

Fernandez, Sergio, and Hal G. Rainey. 2006. "Managing Successful Organizational Change in the Public Sector." *Public Administration Review* 66:168–76.

Finer, Herman. 1941. "Administrative Responsibility in Democratic Government." *Public Administration Review* 1:335–50.

Foucault, Michel. 2000a. *Ethics: Subjectivity, and Truth.* Vol. 1 of *The Essential Works of Foucault 1954–1984,* ed. Paul Rabinow. New York: New Press.

Foucault, Michel. 2000b. *Power.* Vol. 3 of *The Essential Works of Foucault 1954–1984,* ed. James D. Faubion. New York: New Press.

Frederickson, H. George. 1997. *The Spirit of Public Administration.* San Francisco: Jossey-Bass.

French, Peter A. 1983. *Ethics in Government.* Englewood Cliffs, NJ: Prentice-Hall.

Galston, William A. 2002. *Liberal Pluralism: The Implications of Value Pluralism for Political Theory and Practice.* New York: Cambridge University Press.

Gill, Jeff, and Kenneth J. Meier. 2000. "Public Administration Research and Practice: A Methodological Manifesto." *Journal of Public Administration Research and Theory* 10:157–99.

Goodin, Robert E. 2000. "Democratic Deliberation Within." *Philosophy and Public Affairs* 29:81–109.

Gore, Al. 1993. *From Red Tape to Results: Creating a Government That Works Better and Costs Less.* Washington, DC: Government Printing Office.

Gray, John. 1993. *Post-Liberalism: Studies in Political Thought.* New York: Routledge.

———. 1996. *Isaiah Berlin.* Princeton, NJ: Princeton University Press.

———. 2000. *Two Faces of Liberalism.* New York: New Press.

Habermas, Jürgen. 1998. *Between Facts and Norms: Contributions to a Discourse Theory of Law and Democracy.* Cambridge, MA: MIT Press.

Hampshire, Stuart. 1978. "Public and Private Morality." In *Public and Private Morality,* ed. Stuart Hampshire. Cambridge: Cambridge University Press.

———. 1983. *Morality and Conflict.* Cambridge, MA: Harvard University Press.

———. 1989. *Innocence and Experience.* Cambridge, MA: Harvard University Press.

———. 1993. "Liberalism: The New Twist." *New York Review of Books* 40 (August 12): 43–47.

———. 2000. *Justice Is Conflict.* Princeton, NJ: Princeton University Press.

Harold, James. 2003. "Flexing the Imagination." *Journal of Aesthetics and Art Criticism* 61:247–57.

Hausheer, Roger. 1982. Introduction to *Against the Current,* by Isaiah Berlin. New York: Penguin Books.

Heinrich, Carolyn J. 2007. "Evidence-Based Policy and Performance Management: Challenges and Prospects in Two Parallel Movements." *American Review of Public Administration* 37:255–77.

Heraclitus. 2001. *Fragments: The Collected Wisdom of Heraclitus.* Trans. Brooks Haxton. New York: Viking.

Hill, Carolyn J., and Laurence E. Lynn Jr. 2004. "Governance and Public Management, an Introduction." *Journal of Policy Analysis and Management* 23:3–11.

Hobbes, Thomas. 1962. *Leviathan,* ed. Michael Oakeshott. New York: Touchstone.

Hood, Christopher, and Michael Jackson. 1994. "Keys for Locks in Administrative Argument." *Administration and Society* 25:467–88.

Kammen, Michael, ed. 1986. *The Origins of the American Constitution: A Documentary History.* New York: Penguin Books.

Kanigel, Robert. 1997. *The One Best Way: Frederick Winslow Taylor and the Enigma of Efficiency.* New York: Penguin Books.

Kekes, John. 1993. *The Morality of Pluralism.* Princeton, NJ: Princeton University Press.

Lasswell, Harold D. [1930] 1986. *Psychopathology and Politics.* Chicago: University of Chicago Press.

———. 1951. "The Policy Orientation." In *The Policy Sciences: Recent Developments in Scope and Method,* ed. Daniel Lerner and Harold D. Lasswell. Stanford, CA: Stanford University Press.

Levi, Edward H. 1949. *An Introduction to Legal Reasoning.* Chicago: University of Chicago Press.

Lindblom, Charles E. 1990. *Inquiry and Change: The Troubled Attempt to Understand and Shape Society.* New Haven: Yale University Press.

Long, Norton. 1949. "Power and administration." *Public Administration Review* 9:257–64.

Lukes, Stephen. 1989. "Making Sense of Moral Conflict." In *Liberalism and the Moral Life,* ed. Nancy L. Rosenblum. Cambridge, MA: Harvard University Press.

Lynn, Laurence E., Jr. 1996. *Public Management as Art, Science, and Profession.* Chatham, NJ: Chatham House Publishers.

Lynn, Laurence E., Jr., Carolyn J. Heinrich, and Carolyn J. Hill. 2000. "Studying Governance and Public Management: Challenges and Prospects." *Journal of Public Administration Research and Theory* 10:233–61.

Machiavelli, Niccolò. 1950. *The Prince and the Discourses.* New York: Random House.

MacIntyre, Alasdair. 1984. *After Virtue: A Study in Moral Theory.* 2nd ed. Notre Dame, IN: University of Notre Dame Press.

Maynard-Moody, Steven, and Michael Musheno. 2003. *Cops, Teachers, Counselors: Stories from the Front Lines of Public Service.* Ann Arbor: University of Michigan Press.

Mayo, Elton. 1945. *The Social Problems of an Industrial Civilization.* Andover, MA: Andover Press.

Meier, Kenneth J. 1997. "Bureaucracy and Democracy: The Case for More Bureaucracy and Less Democracy." *Public Administration Review* 57:193–99.

Miller, Hugh T. 2003. "The Empirical Discourse of Positivism." Paper presented at the Public Administration Theory Network Conference at the University of Alaska, Anchorage, AK.

Miller, Hugh T., and Charles J. Fox. 2001. "The Epistemic Community." *Administration and Society* 32: 668–85.

Minogue, Kenneth. 1995. *Politics: A Very Short Introduction.* Oxford: Oxford University Press.

Moore, Barrington, Jr. 1993. *Social Origins of Dictatorship and Democracy: Lord and Peasant in the Making of the Modern World.* Boston: Beacon Press.

Nagel, Stuart S., and C. E. Teasley III. 1998. "Diverse Perspectives for Public Policy Analysis." In *Handbook of Public Administration,* ed. Jack Rabin, W. Bartley Hildreth, and Gerald J. Miller. 2nd ed. New York: Marcel Dekker.

Nathan, Richard P. 1995. "Reinventing Government: What Does It Mean?" *Public Administration Review* 55:213–15.

Oakeshott, Michael. 1975. *On Human Conduct.* Oxford: Clarendon Press.

———. 1991. *Rationalism in Politics and Other Essays.* Indianapolis: Liberty Press.

O'Leary, Rosemary. 2006. *The Ethics of Dissent: Managing Guerrilla Government.* Washington, DC: CQ Press.

O'Neill, Timothy D. 1988. "Liberal Constitutionalism and Bureaucratic Discretion." *Polity* 20:371–93.

Osborne, David, and Ted Gaebler. 1993. *Reinventing Government: How the Entrepreneurial Spirit Is Transforming the Public Sector.* New York: Penguin Books.

Osborne, David, and Peter Hutchinson. 2004. *The Price of Government: Getting the Results We Need in an Age of Permanent Fiscal Crisis.* New York: Basic Books.

Osborne, David, and Peter Plastrik. 1997. *Banishing Bureaucracy: The Five Strategies for Reinventing Government.* New York: Addison Wesley.

O'Toole, Laurence J., and Kenneth J. Meier. 2004. "Desperately Seeking Selznick: Cooptation and the Dark Side of Public Management in Networks." *Public Administration Review* 64:681–93.

Overeem, Patrick. 2006. "In Defense of the Dichotomy: A Response to James H. Svara." *Administrative Theory and Praxis* 28:140–47.

———. 2008. "Beyond Heterodoxy: Dwight Waldo and the Politics-Administration Dichotomy." *Public Administration Review* 68:36–45.

Pandey, Sanjay K., and James L. Garnett. 2006. "Exploring Public Sector Communication Performance: Testing a Model and Drawing Implications." *Public Administration Review* 66:37–51.

Parekh, B. 1996. "Moral Philosophy and Its Anti-pluralist Bias." In *Philosophy and Pluralism,* ed. David Archard. Cambridge: Cambridge University Press.

Perelman, Chaïm. 1955. "How Do We Apply Reason to Values?" *Journal of Philosophy* 52:797–802.

———. 1980. *Justice, Law, and Argument: Essays on Moral and Legal Reasoning.* Boston, MA: D. Reidel Publishing Company.

Person, Harlow S. 1972. Foreword to *Scientific Management,* by Frederick Winslow Taylor. Westport, CT: Greenwood Press.

Pesch, Udo. 2005. *The Predicaments of Publicness: An Inquiry into the Conceptual Ambiguity of Public Administration.* Delft, Netherlands: Eburon Academic Publishers.

Pitkin, Hanna Fenichel. 1993. *Wittgenstein and Justice: On the Significance of Ludwig Wittgenstein for Social and Political Thought.* Berkeley: University of California Press.

Poggi, Gianfranco. 1978. *The Development of the Modern State: A Sociological Introduction.* Stanford, CA: Stanford University Press.

Popper, Karl. 1966. *The Open Society and Its Enemies.* Vol. 1 of 2. Princeton, NJ: Princeton University Press.

Putnam, Hilary. 1976. "Literature, Science, and Reflection." *New Literary History* 7:483–91.

Rawls, John. 1996. *Political Liberalism.* New York: Columbia University Press.

Raz, Joseph. 1986. *The Morality of Freedom.* Oxford: Clarendon Press.

Rohr, John A. 1976. "The Study of Ethics in the P.A. Curriculum." *Public Administration Review* 36:398–406.

———. 1986. *To Run a Constitution: The Legitimacy of the Administrative State.* Lawrence, KS: University Press of Kansas.

———. 2002. *Civil Servants and their Constitutions.* Lawrence, KS: University Press of Kansas.

Rorty, Richard. 1982. *Consequences of Pragmatism.* Minneapolis: University of Minnesota Press.

———. 1991. *Objectivity, Relativism, and Truth.* Vol. 1 of *Philosophical Papers.* Cambridge: Cambridge University Press.

———. 2007. *Philosophy as Cultural Politics.* Vol. 4 of *Philosophical Papers,* New York: Cambridge University Press.

Rosenbloom, David H. 1993. "Have an Administrative Rx? Don't Forget the Politics." *Public Administration Review* 53:503–7.

———. 2000a. "Retrofitting the Administrative State to the Constitution: Congress and the Judiciary's Twentieth-Century Progress." *Public Administration Review* 60:39–46.

———. 2000b. *Building a Legislative-Centered Public Administration.* Tuscaloosa, AL: University of Alabama Press.

———. 2007. "Reinventing Administrative Prescriptions: The Case for Democratic-Constitutional Impact Statements and Scorecards." *Public Administration Review* 67:28–39.

Rosenbloom, David H., James D. Carroll, and Jonathan D. Carroll. 2000. *Constitutional Competence for Public Managers: Cases and Commentary.* Itasca, IL: F. E. Peacock Publishers.

Rutgers, Mark R. 2004. "Comparative Public Administration: Navigating Scylla and Charybdis—Global Comparison as a Translation Problem." *Administrative Theory and Praxis* 26:150–68.

Saint-Simon, Henri de. 1964. *Social Organization, the Science of Man and Other Writings.* Trans. Felix Markham. New York: Harper Torchbooks.

Shangraw, R. F., Jr., and Michael M. Crow. 1989. "Public Administration as a Design Science." *Public Administration Review* 49:153–58.

Simon, Herbert A. 1957. *Administrative Behavior: A Study of Decision-Making Processes in Administrative Organization.* 2nd ed. New York: MacMillan.

Skinner, Quentin. 1996. *Reason and Rhetoric in the Philosophy of Hobbes.* Cambridge: Cambridge University Press.

Spicer, Michael W. 1995. *The Founders, the Constitution, and Public Administration: A Conflict in Worldviews.* Washington, DC: Georgetown University Press.

Stillman, Richard J., II. 1998. *Creating the American State: The Moral Reformers and the Modern Administrative World They Made.* Tuscaloosa, AL: University of Alabama Press.

Stivers, Camilla. 2000a. *Bureau Men, Settlement Women: Constructing Public Administration in the Progressive Era.* Lawrence, KS: University Press of Kansas.

———. 2000b. "Resisting the Ascendancy of Public Management: Normative Theory and Public Administration." *Administrative Theory and Praxis* 22:10–23.

———. 2008. "The Significance of *The Administrative State*." *Public Administration Review* 68:53–56.

Stokey, Edith, and Richard Zeckhauser. 1978. *A Primer for Policy Analysis*. New York: W. W. Norton.

Storing, Herbert J., ed. 1985. *The Anti-Federalist*. Chicago: University of Chicago Press.

Strayer, Joseph R. 1970. *On the Medieval Origins of the Modern State*. Princeton, NJ: Princeton University Press.

Sunstein, Cass R. 1993. "On Analogical Reasoning." *Harvard Law Review* 106:741–91.

Svara, James H. 2006. "Complexity in Political-Administrative Relations and the Limits of the Dichotomy." *Administrative Theory and Praxis* 28:121–39.

———. 2008. "Beyond Dichotomy: Dwight Waldo and the Intertwined Politics-Administration Relationship." *Public Administration Review* 68:46–52.

Taylor, Frederick Winslow. [1911] 1998. *The Principles of Scientific Management*. New York: Dover Publications.

Terry, Larry D. 1998. "Administrative Leadership, Neo-Managerialism, and the Public Management Movement." *Public Administration Review* 58:194–200.

Trenchard, John, and Thomas Gordon. 1995. *Cato's Letters*. Ed. Ronald Hamowy. Indianapolis: Liberty Press.

Trevelyan, George Macaulay. 1959. *A Shortened History of England*. Baltimore, MD: Pelican Books.

Urwick, L. 1937. "Organization as a Technical Problem." In *Papers on the Science of Administration,* ed. Luther Gulick and L. Urwick. New York: Institute of Public Administration.

Wagenaar, Hendrik. 1999. "Value Pluralism in Public Administration." *Administrative Theory and Praxis* 21:443–49.

Wagner, Kevin, and Jeff Gill. 2005. "Bayesian Inference in Public Administration Research: Substantive Differences from Somewhat Different Assumptions." *International Journal of Public Administration* 28:5–35.

Waldo, Dwight. [1948] 1984. *The Administrative State: A Study of the Political Theory of American Public Administration*. 2nd ed. New York: Holmes and Meier.

———. 1983. "The Perdurability of the Politics-Administration Dichotomy: Woodrow Wilson and the Identity Crisis in Public Administration." In *Politics and Administration: Woodrow Wilson and American Public Administration,* ed. Jack Rabin and James S. Bowman. New York: Marcel Dekker.

Walzer, Michael. 1973. "Political Action: The Problem of Dirty Hands." *Philosophy and Public Affairs* 2:160–80.

———. 1994. *Thick and Thin: Moral Argument at Home and Abroad*. Notre Dame, IN: University of Notre Dame Press.

Warnock, Mary. 2004. *An Intelligent Person's Guide to Ethics.* New York: Duck Overlook.

Weber, Max. 1946. *Essays in Sociology.* Trans. H. H. Gerth and C. Wright Mills. New York: Oxford University Press.

White, Jay D. 1990. "Images of Administrative Reason and Rationality: The Recovery of Practical Discourse." In *Images and Identities in Public Administration,* ed. Henry D. Kass and Bayard L. Catron. Newbury Park, CA: Sage Publications.

White, Jay D., and Guy Adams. 1995. "Reason and Postmodernity: The Historical and Social Context of Public Administration Research and Theory." *Administrative Theory and Praxis* 17:1–18.

Williams, Bernard. 1978. "Politics and Moral Character." In *Public and Private Morality,* ed. Stuart Hampshire. Cambridge: Cambridge University Press.

———. 1979. Introduction to *Concepts and Categories* by Isaiah Berlin. New York: Viking Press.

Wills, Garry, ed. 1982. *The Federalist Papers by Alexander Hamilton, James Madison, and John Jay.* New York: Bantam Books.

Wilson, James Q. 1989. *Bureaucracy: What Government Agencies Do and Why They Do It.* New York: Basic Books.

Wilson, Woodrow. 1887. "The Study of Administration." *Political Science Quarterly* 2:197–222.

Wolin, Sheldon. 1960. *Politics and Vision: Continuity and Innovation in Western Political Thought.* Boston: Little, Brown.

Index